GRILLING

For Beginners

Table of Contents

About the Author

From the time snow melts in Western New York until it flies again, and often in between, I can be found merrily playing in my back yard at the grill—trying new flavors or cooking up old favorites. But it wasn't always like that. My barbecue efforts began like most folks who crave the amazing taste of a fresh grilled hot dog or hamburger. So, I grabbed a little disposable grill and cooked some up. That was my first mistake. I fell hopelessly in love with results obtained from grilling and barbecue.

I started tinkering, trying new marinades and sauces derived from scratch. As the experimental process continued it had an unusual and unforeseen side effect. Friends started arriving unannounced at my door saying, "Hey, I've got this slab of meat…where's the marinade?" every summer weekend!

Grilling at my home evolved into a time creativity. It's an experience that begs to be shared. I find myself drawn to the welcoming light, its heat, the tempting smells of the fire, and find I want everyone to join me, including you!

I'm Patricia Telesco, and *Grilling for Beginners* is my celebration of an art that I love, and one that I trust will inspire and guide your new exploration in successful and appetizing ways.

Let's get started!

Introduction

"Hana: What on Earth is a 'barbeque'?
Hel: A primitive tribal ritual featuring paper plates, elbows,
flying insects, encrusted meat, hush puppies, and beer.
Hana: I daren't ask what a 'hush puppy' is.
Hel: Don't."

—Rodney William Whitaker ("Trevanian"), *Shibumi*

You've stepped outside and there is something luscious lingering on the wind. It's the smell from your neighbor's barbecue and it makes your stomach growl. You may not know what's on the menu, but you immediately recognize a truly distinctive aroma that people around the world know and love.

Here in America, people grill up food over 3 billion times annually, even during winter months. A barbecue grill is nearly as popular a household item as televisions and computers, with three out of every four homeowners having at least one, if not several, on hand. If you've picked up *Grilling for Beginners* it's likely because you want to join in the fun or learn a little more about the art of barbecue and grilling, and this is a perfect spot to start.

No matter what you see on televised or outdoor cooking competitions, you don't need a Cadillac grill or a great grandfather's rub blend to impress the judges—that is, your friends and family.

Grilling for Beginners is a simple, direct exploration of an ancient method of cooking food polished up for a whole new generation. These pages will be an introduction, mentor and

guide to your grilling efforts. In it, you'll find answers to all of the common questions people have about grilling, including:

- ► How to choose a grill and the tools of your new hobby
- ► How to make and use marinades and rubs that match your recipe
- ► How to whip up great, easy barbecue sauces
- ► How to use smoking wood
- ► How to use a rotisserie
- ► How to manage cooking temperatures for safety

And so much more.

You'll learn about the advantages of gas, wood, and charcoal barbecue, for example. There's also information on food preparation and storage, handy gadgets, and some great recipes so you can start practicing right away.

You can cook anything on your grill that you can in an oven—appetizers, main dishes and even dessert! Preparation and cleanup is no more difficult than following a recipe, doing your dishes and scrubbing the grill as you would any kitchen utensil. It's really that simple!

The best part about barbecue is how pleasurable it becomes once you have a little know-how. Don't build it up with so much mental angst that you stress out the minute you light the grill. Rather, grab a tall, cold beverage, your tools and food, and just enjoy. It's really far easier than you might think, and rather addictive too.

Let's get cooking!

"Even if you're not a great chef, there's nothing to stop you understanding the difference between what tastes good and what doesn't."

—Gerard Depardieu

1

Becoming a Grilling Guru

id you feel that? Right then, when you turned the page. It was a momentous occasion like a disturbance in the Force. You just took your first step toward becoming a grilling guru. Congratulations, Grasshopper!

Don't be daunted—it's a light journey filled with bountiful food, incredible flavors and gatherings of your favorite people. Before you know it, you'll be well on your way to becoming a pit master.

First, let's get you equipped with the basics.

The Lowdown

The Keys to the Grilling Kingdom

At its most basic, there are really only three fundamentals to great grilling:

Time...Temperature...and Smoke.

Of course, we'll go over all of these in detail, but for now, all you need to know is that these are the three elements to master, and you'll be well on your way to becoming a grilling guru.

 Technically speaking, barbecue cooking keeps temperatures between 180 and 250 degrees F. This makes barbecue ideal for tough cuts of meat, because they can stand up to the long cooking times, and even benefit from it.

What's in a Word?

The vast majority of outdoor cooks, including myself, use the terms barbecue and grilling interchangeably. You've probably noticed that this book does so, as well, and will continue to do so throughout. However, this makes hard-core pit masters cringe, because in strictly technical terms, they're not the same—they are actually opposite!

Of course, this is a beginner's guide, so there's no need to get stuck in the weeds— you can decide whether you want to be a stickler once you're a pit master yourself. But here's a little lowdown for you in case you find yourself at an outdoor gathering with a vocabulary snoot:

■ **Barbecue**

The mantra for barbecue is "low, long and slow." You want to infuse a ton of smoke and flavor into the meat without losing moisture. That means employing **indirect heat** so that flames don't touch the food directly. We see this approach with briskets and ribs, for example, and large pieces of meat (like a whole turkey) so that the dish cooks thoroughly inside without burning the exterior.

Shop Talk...

Indirect Heat; N. Cooking with indirect heat means that the gas, charcoal, or wood in your unit is in a different area of the grill than your food. Indirect cooking uses a lid to keep heat and smoke inside the cooking chamber, working a little bit like a convection oven as the warm smoke circulates.

Barbecue is also where you see a lot of smoking wood. It provides heat, flavor, and smoke that creates a distinctive flavor. There are many smoking woods from which to choose. You'll get to read all about those later.

People who focus mostly on barbecue may purchase specially designed units that hold the smoking wood separately with vents that draw the smoke into the main cooking chamber. Some higher end units even have fans for better circulation. However, you can still achieve very good barbecue without those additional accessories.

> **TIP** Barbecue cannot be rushed, and it also requires on-going monitoring for maintaining a ready supply of wood. If you want a fast meal and have a day filled with distractions, grilling is your go-to technique.

▪ Grilling

Most outdoor cooks are well acquainted with grilling, particularly for picnic fare like chicken or burgers. This technique also works very effectively on delicate foods like white fish, fruit, and vegetables.

Where barbecue is low and slow, grilling is fast and hot. The fire goes right under your food, licking the surface and leaving beautiful scorch marks.

> The grill marks on your food occur because the high heat of your unit caramelizes natural sugars in the meat. And while there is some disagreement among professionals about the particulars, this also seals in the juices so that when the meat *rests* after cooking, you have juicier results.

Shop Talk...

Resting; V. When you remove food, particularly meat, from the grill, it needs to settle for a certain amount of time, which is typically designated in the recipe. When you cook meat, the juices move away from the edges. Resting it allows time for that moisture to redistribute throughout the entire cut.

Another distinction between barbecue and grilling is that where barbecue focuses heavily on smoke, grilling often includes a wide variety of sauces and marinades for creating flavor.

Grilling utilizes much higher heats than barbecue and gets the vast majority of its flavor profiles from the sauces, spices, or marinades used before and during the cooking process.

And the Winner is...

So which is better: barbecue or grilling? That depends on who you ask. Personal taste plays a role in that answer, as well as how much time you have to dedicate to outdoor cooking. The recipes in this book rely more heavily on grilling for a variety of reasons, chief among them the fact that this is for beginners. Many people don't have time for long smoking processes, and grilling is a tad easier than barbecuing. Once you're comfortable with the grilling process, you can add smoking as a technique to diversify your flavors later on. So there really isn't a "winner"—it's all part of the process.

THE TAKEAWAY

▶ Barbecue is a slow process that uses indirect heat and smoke to cook and flavor food, often large or tough cuts.

▶ Grilling is a fast, hot process suited for more delicate foods, or those items whose flavors benefit from direct flame

"Fads are orderly. Food carts and fires aren't. Feeding the world could be a delicious mess, full of diverse flavors and sometimes good old-fashioned smoke."

—Tyler Cowen,
An Economist Gets Lunch: New Rules for Everyday Foodies

Choosing a Grill

I t's rather hard to set up your cooking station without
equipment, so this chapter will introduce you to all your
grilling options so that you can shop intelligently. The most
important decision that you'll make for your new hobby is what
type of grill you want. That choice changes your recipe selections as well as how you prepare your cooking space.   *continued...*

Author's Aside

I vividly remember the first year I got a bonus check. I knew immediately I wanted to use it for a GOOD grill, but choosing wasn't as easy as I thought. The options of brands, designs, and functions were pretty impressive. We ended up with what I call a hybrid: it uses gas, charcoal, or wood, and has an offset smoker. Barbecue. Heaven.

Gas Grills

Why Go with Gas?

When friends ask about the best type of grill for a novice, I recommend gas. Charcoal and wood lovers, don't despair—it's just that the convenience of gas is conducive to learning. 70% of home barbecue sales are for gas grills, probably because of their simplicity, evenness/control of temperature and one-button ignitions.

Grilling with gas is by far the most popular choice among consumers. It's easier to use because of the evenness of heat control and the fact that you can light it with a push of a button. Nonetheless, many grillers argue that charcoal imparts better flavor.

Benefits and Drawbacks

Gas is a great time saver for people with crazy schedules. Rather than waiting on the charcoal to get to temperature, your grill gets hot very quickly. That's not the only savings—where a bag of charcoal lasts for one or two uses depending on the size, a propane tank burns for about 20 hours. That's a lot of outdoor cooking! Cleanup is also easier with gas—no messy ashes that seem to leave fingerprints everywhere.

Does that mean gas grilling is "all that?" No. You cannot nudge flavors out of a gas grill that you can from charcoal and wood. Additionally the typical gas grill costs more than charcoal, and many gas grills have no equipment for smoking foods. When you do find a brand with smoker boxes, you're looking at a greater investment. That means focusing on your barbecue budget from the get-go (keeping in mind that you'll also need tools.)

Special Feature...

The World's Most Expensive Grill

The most expensive grills in the world are the Kalamazoo Outdoor Gourmet grills. They offer a hybrid system—both charcoal and gas, with infrared burners and a rotisserie. As of 2014 this Epicurean delight cost approximately $20,000—yes, really. There is a smaller version for the budget-minded consumer that costs about $12,000, and if you're feeling middle of the road you can spend just $17,000.

Choosing a Gas Grill

When you walk into any decent hardware store it becomes readily apparent that there are nearly as many models of outdoor cookers as there are automobiles. As a beginner, focus on the performance of a grill over extravagant options. All those bells and whistles are tempting, but they're also costly. Stick to the fundamentals with your first grill. What you want is a barbecue that offers solid construction, the right-size cooking surface for your needs, and one that receives high consumer ratings.

In fact, before you even step out your door for shopping, get on the internet and read some consumer reviews. These are gold! By reading a handful you'll notice some trends—where people had problems (like difficulty with assembly) and what they like best about the grill (like an exterior thermometer).

Three Key Considerations

There are three things you want to consider in your gas grill:

Size...Shape/Materials...and Functionality.

KEY POINT

The important things to remember when buying a gas grill is its size (so it can feed all of your family and friends), the shape and material from which it's made (for longevity), and how well it works based on consumer ratings.

■ **Size Matters**

Think about how many people you anticipate feeding from your grill. Hint: this isn't a time to think BIG. When you're cooking for up to four people you only need about 400 square inches. More than that and you're wasting not only space but fuel. By comparison, if you want to feed 40 people you need about 1100+ square inches (that's for basic burgers, folks) so leave that effort to caterers.

TIP If you live in an apartment, you already see your problem: Space is tight! Some complexes don't even allow any type of grill so check your rental agreement first. If that's a "go"—don't forget you can make food in rounds—think first in first out. Those early guests take their food, sit and chat while others get their first serving. This approach takes pressure off the cook and still gets everyone fed.

Note that the advice about choosing size applies to charcoal and wood, too. Be reasonable about where you're taking this project, including thinking toward the future. "Buy once, buy right" is a great mantra.

■ **Materials**

Having owned several grills in my lifetime, I like iron, stainless, and cast aluminum. All three resist the wear-and-tear of the elements (particularly if you get a decent cover). Yes, all three cost a little more but you'll get far more longevity out of them. More importantly, they perform better than cheaper versions. At the end of the day you want a grill that makes great food and that you don't have to replace annually.

Definitely read the product information during your shopping. Some things that appear to be stainless steel are not. Real stainless steel uses various alloys that make it resistant to rust, tough enough to withstand high cooking temperatures and gives it a finish that won't be affected by harsh cleaners. These three benefits outweigh a little extra cleaning to keep that shine alive.

TIP You can tell if a grill is a knock-off stainless steel if it's got magnetic properties. True stainless steel does not hold magnets. It also shows fingerprints readily and requires special cleaning products.

■ **Functionality**

So how well does it work? You definitely want a grill that generates over 30,000 BTUs for all-purpose cooking. If you don't, you'll be frustrated with your beginner's efforts and see poor results. Another key feature for functionality is flexibility with placement. A grill on wheels rocks, because you can move it where you want for any occasion. You can also transfer it into a holding facility for off-season protection.

Another feature to watch for is metal deflectors that rest over the gas. These distribute heat evenly throughout the grill, meaning your food gets done on time, at the same time. Remember when Mom or Dad managed to have everything in a meal ready at once? Prepare to amaze and amuse!

Certainly there are other features you may like. I prefer a grill that has a built in temperature gauge, for example. Some have windows that let you keep an eye on your meal's progress. Really, it's up to you. Each additional gadget raises your price, so you need to find your own balance.

Using the Grill

Rule number one: do not start your grill before reading the manual.

Please read that rule again—it's not optional.

WARNING!

No matter how long you've been grilling, each barbecue is different, so for safety, when you set up a new grill always follow the manufacturer's directions carefully.

Never use your grill in an enclosed area. Turn on the gas with the hood open, then use the ignition or a match. If you must use a match, get the long-handled kind and wear an oven mitt.

If you do not follow the preceeding warnings, your result will eventually be people flambé—serious burns and serious medical bills if you're lucky enough to survive a barbecue explosion. **Safety always comes first.**

Author's Aside

This particular piece of advice comes to you by way of rather embarrassing experience. I had singed eyebrows and bangs for weeks because I didn't follow that simple two-step safety feature. I was lucky and wasn't seriously burned, but I almost became one of the dozens of Americans that die every year in barbecue accidents.

At this point you can let the grill run on high to clean the cooking surface. Adjust the temperature afterward to the recipe's instructions and go forward from there.

TIP Gas grills can get too hot. If you find your unit running over temperature, you can try turning down the amount of propane from the tank. Alternatively, put a fireproof wedge in the lid to keep it open a crack. A closed grill is a hot grill and it cooks very fast while an open grill cooks slower.

■ The Temperature

Everything you cook in the oven has temperatures that either make or break your recipe. The grill is no different. When you cook fish on a gas grill, cook it over a medium fire with seasoned oil. Chicken is a little more durable so you can work with medium to hot fire, which is also true for pork. Steak likes high heat for charring, and vegetables prefer low heat so they can absorb flavors.

Cleanup

Sadly, grills do not clean themselves, so you'll have to do it. It's important to keep your grill clean for on-going food safety. After cooking, turn the burners up to high for about seven minutes and let excess food or grease burn off. Afterward, use a sturdy wire brush to scrub any excess off of the steel grates. If your grill has ceramic, use just a regular soft cloth with soap and water.

There is no short-changing in cleaning your grill. Just like your kitchen countertop or dishes, the cleanliness of your cooking surface equates directly to food safety.

Storage

If you're not keen on barbecuing in inclement weather, you'll probably want to stash your unit away during seasons where the weather is particularly bad. To get it ready for storage, wash out your grill completely. You may need wire to clean out the gas outlets. Afterward, apply a coating of oil. The easy way to do this is with regular cooking spray. Then, heat the grill to about 275 degrees and let it cook for an hour. This will create a protective surface for storage.

Once cool, continue cleaning the exterior. Shut off and remove the propane tank. Store this outdoors. It should not be in a closed space. Wrap the gas fittings using a garbage bag or plastic wrap so that bugs and dust don't clog the holes. Cover and put wherever you store your other seasonal items.

Author's Aside

Successful Grilling

Here are a few basic rules for grilling success:

1. *Gas grills will sometimes flare up. If you leave a spot on your grill that's empty, you can easily move the food to avoid burning. Just keep your lid open until the fire calms down.*

2. *Never leave your grill unattended. That "one minute" to check football scores can easily distract you until your food turns to charcoal.*

3. *If you like sweet sauces, these are one of the biggest causes of grill fires. Keep your temperature controls under 250 degrees.*

4. *Check your fuel levels. Nothing messes up a recipe like only half-finishing it because you ran out of gas in the middle of cooking.*

Charcoal Grills

So, maybe a gas grill isn't quite your cup of tea? You want to jump straight into the bolder, more flavorful (and less costly) arena of barbecue—charcoal. You got it! The nifty part about charcoal grilling is that it makes its own smoke, and creates a distinct flavor. Briquettes naturally burn hot, so you'll have no trouble keeping your meats juicy by searing. Also, many charcoal grills are suited to wood, for those who want to do traditional smoking.

 KEY POINT

While charcoal is a little messier than gas, and less predictable temperature-wise, it imparts a natural, smoky flavor that plain gas grilling cannot.

There has certainly been plenty of heated (pun intended) debate over whether charcoal is better than gas. I confess, it is fun learning the art of making an effective cooking fire with charcoal or wood. However, the process isn't as forgiving gas. You don't have any real predictability and cleanup takes longer. But if you don't mind a little inconvenience and giving your grill more attention, you'll love charcoal's great smoky flavor.

Choosing a Charcoal Grill

As with a gas grill, you have a lot of elements in considering your new purchase. I advise buying the best grill you can within your budget. You don't want to replace your equipment every season. That means you want something that resists rust and has a solid gauge metal. You also have to decide if you want something portable or built in. A built-in grill will be more expensive and you can't take it with you on camping trips or if you move, but they certainly make a distinctive landscape feature for entertaining.

Either way, there are features that make or break a charcoal grill:

- **Convenience**
- **Cooking Grate Materials**
- **Features**
- **Guarantees**

Unlike gas, you can't just turn on a knob and keep a charcoal fire going. Look for a unit that makes adding more charcoal safe and easy, preferably by a separate door. That way you don't have to move the food or the grates. This basic concept applies to ashes too. If you build up too much ash, the fire won't burn properly. Removable ash pans are a fantastic ally.

The grates on charcoal grills may be iron, stainless steel, or porcelain. I'm a fan of iron, because it's durable, heats wonderfully, gives you rockin' hash marks and it's affordable.

TIP Season your cast iron grates when you first start using your unit, and at least once per year thereafter. This keeps food from sticking and keeps rust at bay. Begin by washing the grates with soap and water and let dry completely. Next, coat them with vegetable shortening and place them on the grill for 15 minutes on low. Once cool, you're ready to cook. Do not scrape the surfaces after cooking, rather heat them on high and clean them before the next cookout.

Many manufacturers are rapidly ramping up the features they offer on charcoal grills. Some have rotisseries, built-in heat monitors, and more—but as with gas, each additional item increases your costs. It might be smart to get a unit that has separate add-ons so you can purchase them as your budget allows.

Preparation, Cleaning and Storage

After setting up your grill according to manufacturer's instructions you'll need charcoal. Consider lump charcoal: It doesn't contain a lot of fillers and offers greater heat control than briquettes.

Next comes the accelerant. Some people use old-fashioned paper to get the coals started while others use lighting fluid. The advantage of paper is that it doesn't smell like chemicals and leaves the food's flavor untainted. Regardless, never begin cooking until the coals turn completely white. Spread them out evenly in the bottom of the unit and place the grates on top. You can oil the grates lightly to prevent food from sticking.

Once the grill cools completely, you can wipe out the remaining charcoal debris and wash the outside of the grill using plain soap and water. This will deter flare-ups.

WARNING!

Charcoal should never be used in an enclosed area. It is also important to make sure your grill is completely extinguished before you store it. If the coals rekindle, they give off lethal carbon monoxide. Last year, almost twenty Americans died from carbon monoxide poisoning caused by their barbecues. When in doubt, leave the unit in open air until the next day, then tackle cleanup.

Storing a charcoal grill is similar to storing a gas unit. Clean it out, give it a light coating of oil, cover it, and put it away. Don't forget to cover any excess charcoal too. An airtight storage bin does nicely. It keeps the briquettes dry and ensures you'll be able to use them again next season.

Tips and Tricks

Here are a few tricks to improve your charcoal cooking:

♦ If you want to bake on charcoal, stoneware pans work great. Just remember that most baked goods take a little longer to finish on a grill than in the oven.

♦ Should your outdoor adventure include rain, you'll have to adjust the heat in the unit before adding more charcoal. Avoid opening the lid when possible, as that reduces the interior temperature.

♦ On windy days endeavor to place your grill in some area that offers a wind break to keep temperature even.

♦ Don't put food too close together on the grill surface. It needs air space in order to cook evenly.

♦ Keep a spray bottle handy to tame the occasional flare-up before it damages your food.

♦ If you're planning on kebobs and have wooden skewers, soak them in water, juice, or wine for a half hour before spearing and cooking the food. This keeps them from burning.

Wood & Pit Grills

Cooking over wood isn't much different than using charcoal. Really, the biggest variation is the resulting flavor and cooking time. Once wood turns white, it's ready—then it's just a matter of learning the subtleties of your fire. Remember that rain and wind affect temperature and you have to adjust your recipes accordingly.

A few considerations with wood and pit barbecues: One, the cost of fire wood may be higher than propane or charcoal in the long haul, particularly if you're looking for good smoking wood. Second, wood burns more quickly than charcoal and propane. You'll need a ready supply if you're cooking larger cuts or whole birds. Finally, the pit barbecue benefits from a rotisserie setup so that you can evenly heat and baste your food, keep it away from direct flame and easily replenish the wood.

Choosing a Wood or Pit Barbecue

Barbecue pits have become a very popular design element in landscaping. In fact, it can even improve the value of your home. There are pits pre-designed for a variety of outdoor settings to which you can add seating and seasonal decorations for ambiance. Stone and concrete units not only look lovely but endure the outdoor environment for a long time. Concrete has a more modern appeal while stone feels rustic. Avoid a cheap metal pit, as they rust and don't last for very long.

TIP Fire pits can be fueled by propane, wood, or charcoal. If you want heat, wood is the best option. Yes, it takes a little more effort to set up and keep the pit burning, but the aesthetic value and warmth far outshine propane.

Unless you're a professional stone layer, its best to buy a pre-made fire pit or hire a contractor who insures their work against defects. You will have to check the fire codes in your area regarding the pit's placement. As a general rule, clear a 10-foot radius all around the pit of anything flammable, including vegetation.

WARNING!

Look up! Are there any low trees in the area where you're planning your pit assembly? Design experts such as Dan Fritschen (*Remodel or Move*) suggest that the pit remain about 30 feet away from the nearest overhead limb.

Preparation, Cleaning and Storage

Preparing your cooking surface isn't that different if you're using grates. Make sure the grate is placed properly and lightly oiled before you light your fire. Have a hook or tongs that you can use for moving the grate safely if you need to add more wood (unless the construction has a side feeder, which certainly makes things easier). Other useful tools for your fire pit include skillets, pots, pans, and a **Dutch oven**.

Shop Talk...

Dutch Oven; N. The Dutch oven first appeared around the 1700s. This large pot has thick walls and are usually made from iron, although some manufacturers create clay or ceramic versions. It became popular because of its tremendous versatility—it's suitable for stew, soup, baking, roasts, frying, and of course barbecue!

One thing I recommend with a fire pit is getting a tripod. You can hang various sized pots from this up away from the direct flame, making it ideal for soup and stew. Another great tool is a rotisserie—you can get one that's manual but many offer the option of electric so you don't have to sit and spin all day.

How you clean and store your pit depends on whether you have a permanent fixture or a portable pit set up, and the base materials from which it's made. Treat metal pits as you would a gas or charcoal grill—keep them clean and protect them from the elements during the off season. Built-in pits may have other instructions for treating the stone, cleaning, and weatherization. Check your owner's manual or contractor's instructions and follow them for maximum pit longevity.

KEY POINT

Wood and Barbecue Pits make a great landscaping feature that can increase the value of your home. The only downside is that wood costs more than charcoal.

Tips and Tricks

♦ Always use hardwood. It's got burn longevity and a savory aromatic profile. Avoid any wood with resin because you don't want that sticky residue in your food. You do not have to use just one type of wood, either; mix and match for an array of flavor layers.

♦ Whenever possible, start your fire without chemicals. Try paper, dry leaves, small dry branches, fire starter sticks or charcoal. The flavor of your food and the way your grill smells will both benefit from the extra effort.

♦ Be patient. You need the wood to get small glowing embers similar to charcoal or your food is likely to burn.

♦ After you're done cooking go ahead and add some more wood. You can sit and enjoy the fire while you have dessert!

Special Feature...

Other Forms of Barbecue Cooking

As you might imagine, this is just the tip of the flame when it comes to barbecue methods and units. Some others include plank grilling, where the food cooks on cedar or other aromatic planks that infuse special flavors, and infrared grilling that uses high temperatures. In terms of alternative grill setups there's the Hibachi from Japan, an open top metal system that uses charcoal, the Adogan fire pot from West Africa made from earthenware, and the Chinese hot pot made from metal and kept warm at the table, just to name a few.

THE TAKEAWAY

▶ Gas grills rule the consumer market because they're easy and offer even cooking temperatures.

▶ Size, shape and materials are three important keys to selecting the right grill for your home and lifestyle.

▶ No matter the grill, cleaning and maintaining it properly is essential for food safety and the longevity of your unit.

▶ Charcoal is unpredictable compared to gas but it imparts a distinct flavor and aroma to your food.

▶ Wood imparts great flavor, and having a barbecue pit as part of the landscape is an easy way to bring a social element to your backyard.

"Don't underestimate the importance of having enough room to work. Grilling is much more relaxing when you are not trying to juggle a whole collection of plates and bowls as you do it."

—Bobby Flay, celebrity chef

Have Pot Holder, Will Travel

Tool Time

It's **tool time!** Just like any other form of cooking barbecue has some tools that help you create a safe and sumptuous meal. Not every single tool in this chapter is necessary at the start, and you probably have several items in your kitchen already (i.e. you don't need to dedicate another one just to your grill). The most important thing is that you choose the right implements for your style of barbecue and your grilling unit.

continued...

Effective tool selection makes for more success with your barbecue efforts. Buying the right tools will also support food and fire safety.

Apron

Barbecue can be quite a messy pastime. It doesn't matter how diligently you keep up with cleaning your grill, there is always the chance of smoke, dirt, and food bits finding their way onto your clothing. Barbecue can create pretty stubborn stains, so an apron saves a lot of laundry.

There are all manner of styles and features for aprons from the very basic white butcher style to one that's full length with pockets and an adjustable neckline. I recommend something heavy duty that withstands grease and repeated washing. An apron with pockets does double duty for carrying your spices or small tools. This is not a moment to get caught up in a fashion craze—go for utility. Dark colored aprons hide stains better.

After wearing the apron, spray some stain cleaner on the tough spots before washing it. Soak the apron in warm soapy water, then put it in the washing machine (do not use hot water or stains get stuck in the fibers). You want to keep the apron separate from whites or any fabrics that absorb grease too. Put your dryer on low, or better yet, air dry the apron in open air to keep stains from setting.

Cutting Board

Once upon a time, the standard cutting board in most homes was made from a piece of hardwood. These days, you have a lot more options, including plastic, ceramic and bamboo. Personally, I prefer bamboo. It is highly sustainable and easily grown in a chemical-free environment. For the "green" homes out there, bamboo makes environmental sense. Studies show that bamboo does not absorb as much liquid as traditional wood, which also may make it more hygienic. By comparison, traditional wood cutting boards are a little easier on your culinary knives, because they are softer than bamboo by about 20 percent.

TIP You can extend the longevity of a wooden cutting board by cleaning, drying and oiling it after every use. This deters warping and stains. NEVER put a wooden cutting board in a dishwasher. In terms of preferred woods, maple seems to be the timber of choice for many quality cutting boards.

Plastic cutting boards were, for a time, all the rage but it turns out that chefs no longer readily recommend them. While they last long and endure the wear and tear of the dishwasher, knives leave small scratches in the surface that make perfect hidey-holes for bacteria. Glass cutting boards are also at the bottom of a cook's list because they really hurt good cooking blades.

TIP Keep three cutting boards in your home: One for breads, fruits and vegetables, one for raw fish, meat and poultry, and one for cooked proteins. That way, you're not interrupting your cooking process to wash cutting boards.

For an all-purpose board, consider the Epicurean brand. This company specializes in products that have non-porous faces, that go in the dishwasher safely and that won't hurt your cutting knives. The material is an amalgam of wood fibers and resin that was originally created for skating parks!

KEY POINT *Different cutting boards suit different purposes. A wooden one is great for vegetables and breads, plastic for meat, poultry, and fish, and an Epicurean board for when you want an all-purpose, durable board.*

Dispensers

Kitchen dispensers come in various materials including glass, plastic, stainless, and porcelain. They also have different configurations including pump pour, **sauce guns**, and squeeze bottles.

Shop Talk...

Sauce Gun; N. Sauce guns look a lot like the guns used for caulking. They're designed in stainless steel with a plastic sauce holder that snaps in place. The beauty of a sauce gun is that it gives you portion control. The gun has specific increments marked off (such as 1 ounce, or ½ ounce) so you'll never have to worry about that accidental huge blob of catsup, barbecue sauce, or salad dressing on top of your dish again.

A lot of grillers prefer plastic squeeze bottles. They won't break on the concrete should you knock or drop them and you can see how much sauce you have inside. Glass is nice in that it doesn't hold smells like plastic does over time, but it's a little more risky for outdoor events. Pump pour bottles are great for when you have a serve-yourself style buffet

Fire Extinguisher

When you think about safe barbecuing, a fire extinguisher should be one of your first purchases. But don't just buy it and keep it near the grill—learn how to use it effectively!

Since oil sometimes flares up, and you may use an accelerant from time to time, I recommend purchasing a combination Type A and B, with A for ordinary combustibles and B for flammable liquids. When you buy it, make sure you can lift and move it easily in an emergency situation—some of those suckers are heavy!

Consider rechargeable extinguishers with indicators showing when your supply gets low. Refilling saves money over disposable extinguishers in the long run.

Grill Press

Sometimes called a burger press or steak weight, a grill press goes on top of food as a means of shortening cooking time and adding grill marks. Made from cast iron with a handle, you heat up the press when you pre-heat your grill. Once the grill is up to temperature, just move the press aside until you have your food in place, then put the press on top. This cooks your chosen items from both sides. Afterward, cool the press and season it in the same manner as a grill grate (see Chapter 2).

Hand Protection

Fire = burns. It's a very simple equation. That means you need some decent oven or grill mitts to safeguard yourself while cooking. Hint: flimsy, cheap mitts are not the answer to avoiding burns.

What exactly should you look for in a grilling mitt? You want something that can go through the washer (they will get saucy), that's durable, and that fits properly. If you can hold your grilling tools and manipulate them easily, that's a good mitt fit. I suggest one that goes beyond your wrist for maximum reach and protection. Now all this sensibility doesn't mean losing style. Hand protection comes in numerous colors and patterns so you can match it up to your picnic ware or exterior landscaping accents.

 Hand protection is every bit as important as your other safety precautions, including the fire extinguisher and thermometer.

Mixing and Storage Bowls

This may be a no-brainer as most people have some type of mixing and storage bowls kicking around the kitchen. Nevertheless, sometimes they break, or tops get lost and you're off to the store again.

Grilling and culinary bowls come in various materials including plastic, wood, copper, glass, steel, and ceramic. If you do a lot of outdoor preparation, I suggest looking for a sturdy bowl that won't shatter if you accidentally drop it. Plastic food storage units serve both purposes—mixing, storage, and **marinating** your food.

 Shop Talk...

·Marinating; V. Soaking any type of food in a liquid (wine, juice, salad dressing, beer, etc.) for a pre-determined amount of time. This imparts flavor and tenderizes your meat selections.

Special Feature...

Grilling—Everything Old is New Again

Brazier grills became popular in the 1940s and 50s, inspired by a vast exodus to the suburbs and people's interest in outdoor cooking. The Brazier grill had wheels and a metal pan for holding charcoal. They weren't consistent, but were a fun innovation to show off to family and friends. What most people didn't know, however, is that Brazier's design had ancient roots.

An archaeology dig in Turkey found earthen kiln barbecues similar to Braziers that were over 2,000 years old. The grills were handmade, portable and affordable to even the homes of local fishers.

Thermometer

Grilling without a thermometer is like trying to finely slice a steak using a sharp knife…while blindfolded. While some cooks swear you can tell when meat is done by touch, it is not a safe cooking practice. Undercooked food can lead to food poisoning. A thermometer takes away the worry and gives you greater control over your recipe.

WARNING! The U.S. Centers for Disease Control (CDC) warns that around 130,000 Americans end up in the hospital due to foodborne sickness every year. Don't skip food safety—get an oven-proof thermometer for meats and keep a reliable digital thermometer to check the temperature inside the grill.

Timer

Time can get away from you easily when you're entertaining at the grill. Look for a timer that's easy to understand. The instructions shouldn't read like a stereo manual and the numbers should be easy to read even from a slight angle.

If you're cooking several things at the same time, look for a "multi event" timer. Depending on the brand, you can find some that track up to four or more dishes simultaneously. A timer with a waterproof feature is also useful in the case of unexpected rain.

Grilling Utensils

Now for some fun. It's time to put your barbecue tool kit together. This list contains my suggestions for the best tools for beginners. Good tools mean better cooking results, too. Don't forget: Buy once, buy right.

Tongs

Let's start with tongs. You want something that grabs hold of the food and transfers it to the plate without having something fall in the grill or (egad!) on the ground to a hungry pup. A good set of tongs will grip without piercing, and are long enough to reach the far corners of your grill. Just as when shopping for barbecue shears, make sure they fit your hand and aren't too heavy.

Barbecue tools that you use to reach, move, or serve food should have long, comfortable handles so you can safely get to all corners of your grill and maneuver food effectively.

Spatula

Many of the rules for tongs apply to spatulas—think long handles and comfortable grips. Now, manufacturers have designed some spatulas with tons of bells and whistle including bottle openers, which do nothing for the tool's actual function, which is to turn your food without it falling apart.

Fork

A long-handled, two-prong fork is another good tool for placing, turning and retrieving food. Don't worry—despite the old barbecue myth, a fork will not hurt the juiciness of your meat. Choose a fork with long, comfortable handles.

TIP Another barbecue myth is that salting meat before you grill it makes it dry. Actually, if you use coarse salt, cracked pepper, and any other preferred spices just before cooking, it acts like a rub and creates a nice savory crust.

Brushes/Scrapers

Before you buy anything, check the grill's owner manual to see what the manufacturer recommends for cleaning utensils. A brush-scraper combo harms certain grates, particularly porcelain. A copper brush is a better choice, and very inexpensive. Bear in mind that this tool alone won't keep your grill wholly clean. It's still important to regularly wash your grates to remove any small bits of food that could house bacteria.

Shears

Shears are a great addition to your grilling tool set. You can use them for everything from separating chicken parts to snipping fresh herbs and cutting open your barbecue charcoal. When shopping look for shears that have good edges, feel good in your hands, and that clean up easily. You can get fancy, but that doesn't always mean better.

Author's Aside

I am not a big fan of pull-apart shears. These can pop apart and jump out of your grasp. Spring-loaded handled blades are also sneaky, and managing them for larger culinary efforts is difficult for people with weak or small hands. Always test kitchen shears on a variety of materials before buying to make sure they're comfortable and cut smoothly. I recommend the Shun Classic line—they offer a bit of everything, have rave consumer reviews, and cost under $50.

Mop

The cotton mop has been used in barbecue mostly for roasting meat over a pit with smoking wood. The long handle makes it easy to apply all manner of sauces. This is not a necessary utensil if you don't plan on open pit or spit pit grilling. You can opt for some type of smaller application tool like the brush featured in the above picture.

Knife

I confess, I'm a bit picky when it comes to knives. I prefer buying one good set and treating it with proper respect for a very long time over a cheaper option. A good barbecue knife set should include one serrated blade, which you use for meat carving and slicing bread and vegetables. Your "go to" knife is a chef's knife—it's a multi-tasker so if you can only buy one good knife, splurge here. A boning knife slides into tight spaces in fish and meat for easy disassembly, and a paring knife works for vegetable preparation. If you have all of these, add a sharpening steel to your shopping list and learn to use it. This extends the useful life of your blades considerably.

Some of the better brands on the market include Wusthof, Ginsu (yes, really—a lot of bang for your buck here), Chicago Cutlery, Henckels, and Cuisinart.

Wire Basket

Wire baskets are designed for baby or chopped vegetables so they get grilled taste without falling into the fire. When you pick out a basket, try to find one that's non-stick, that fits on your grill with the lid closed, and that's dishwasher safe. Also review the size of the holes—some baskets aren't designed for tiny morsels.

Special Feature...

Barbecue Tool Development

It was the late 1950s in America when manufacturers realized that we'd caught the outdoor cooking bug in a big way. They began promoting grilling necessities for people who wanted to impress friends and neighbors with their savvy toys. It didn't take long for market expansion, with people caving to all sorts of marketing and buying barbecue tools from corn holders to novel seasoning shakers or full grilling kits. One set from 1970s was a mid-line offering called the Cheftender Ranger. It included a spatula, scraper, fork and carving knife.

Wood Chips

For the beginner thinking of smoking foods, you'll be happy to know that there is a whole chapter devoted to smoking later in this book, but even if you don't plan to dive into smoking any time soon, you should at least understand the importance of wood chips to an outdoor chef's *mise en place*.

It's tremendously fun to mix and match woods for unique aromas and flavors. Some woods have a very mild, but distinct smoke. Cherry is one that (as you might expect) is also fruity, which makes it a great choice for poultry. Apple carries a similar profile. Try it with fish just to change things up a bit. Oak and hickory create stronger smokes, without the sweetness of fruit, for things like bacon, pork, and beef (if you want a sweet oak, try wine barrel oak chips.) When looking for an "in your face" smoke flavor and aroma, use mesquite. This is the hands-down choice for Texas style brisket.

 KEY POINT

Barbecue wood can create subtle or bold flavors. Take care in picking wood suitable for your recipe. Delicate food requires a gentle smoking hand or you'll overwhelm natural flavors.

THE TAKEAWAY

▶ Select your tools of the trade wisely. This improves your overall success and safety.

▶ Pick a cutting board for your barbecue that suits the type of food you're serving. Use wood for bread and vegetables, and plastic for meats.

▶ Always use hand protection when working your grill. This is a matter of safety, as is having a functional fire extinguisher and accurate thermometer.

▶ For reaching, moving, and serving food, use long tools with comfortable handles.

▶ Wood choices for smoked dishes should reflect the recipe and the delicateness or robustness of the main offering.

"When I figured out how to work my grill, it was quite a moment. I discovered that summer is a completely different experience when you know how to grill."

—Taylor Swift, country music star

4

Getting Ready

The End of the Beginning

Hopefully by now you've got a grill and your basic tools. There's still a little preparation work, however (you knew that was coming didn't you?). Getting everything ready for your barbecue is a very important step in the process. Part of what we'll review here is basic food safety, which when working outdoors becomes a little trickier. This chapter also introduces some information on setting up your grilling area for greatest effectiveness. Don't worry—if your grill is already assembled, you've done the hard part already.

Location, Location, Location

While there is nothing wrong with putting a picnic table in the grass, that is not the place for your barbecue grill. The National Fire Protection Agency recommends placing your grill well away from the house and any flammable objects like wooden handrails. You want the grill on an even, fireproof surface (like concrete).

TIP If you don't have a concrete pad somewhere outdoors, an alternative is using pavers or bricks of the same size. Hunt down the flattest spot in your yard then place the stones adjacent to each other. Stand on them to test the overall surface balance.

Fire Tending 101

Step one before you even consider starting the grill, is to read your owner's manual. A lot of people skip this step and miss key points for operating their barbecue properly. The information in that book is specific to your unit. Even if you've grilled before, when you first use a new grill, you need get to know its peculiar quirks—how quickly it lights, how fast it comes up to temperature, how the grates go in and out, etc. If you do not have an owner's manual, you can often obtain them online.

If you have chosen to go with a charcoal grill make sure to ONLY use paper or charcoal fluid as an accelerant. Charcoal grills cause more fires than gas, so stay on your toes. Once started, do not add charcoal fluid to the fire as the stream can transport a spark back up into the can. An electric charcoal starter is a good alternative that offers more safety.

WARNING! Grills start fires every year because people don't look carefully at the location. Look for vines, trees, etc. that might catch a spark. Also remember that people will be milling around your barbecue party. You want plenty of walk space so no guests, pets, or children accidentally get burnt.

For those who went with a gas grill, check the propane hose at the start of your season. You can do this easily by opening the flow regulator and applying soapy water to the length of the hose. If there is an outflow, it will bubble and/or smell like gas. It is dangerous to use the grill before replacing this part if it shows signs of leaking.

If your grill has been in storage, look in the little holes on the gas outlets, in the valves and even the knobs. If bugs or dirt cause blockage in these places, it can result in gas getting redirected, which can cause fires.

Don't skimp on safety measures. They are the most important part of your preparation process so that everyone can have a wonderful gathering without accidents.

Indoors and Out

Barbecue is a little different than making your Sunday meal on a stove. Preparation takes place both inside and out. Inside, make sure your kitchen is clean and organized for the task at hand. That means getting out measuring tools, mixing bowls, and all the recipe components.

The French call this part of the process *mise en place*, which means putting everything in place. The idea is getting each ingredient for your recipe and placing them in the order in which they come in the food prep process. This has a ton of advantages, not least of which is the assurance that you have everything on hand and won't have to run to the supermarket mid-recipe. As you use an ingredient, put it away. This avoids missing a key step or accidentally using the wrong ingredient (like salt for sugar).

You can apply *mise en place* to your outdoor grilling area too. Are chairs set up for comfortable discussions? Can people walk easily around tables, chairs, and the cooking area? Have you got enough tableware? What about a cooler for beverages, umbrellas for shade, some insect candles, and a garbage can for fast clean up? You don't want to be fussing with all these details when guests arrive so get it all out of the way ahead of time. Doing so allows you to give your full attention to your barbecue until you serve the food and get to enjoy the fruit of your labors.

Planning and preparing ahead gives you much more time for entertaining guests. It also keeps your attention on cooking the food perfectly.

Author's Aside

As someone not overly fond of the smell of citronella, I take a cue from history and use basil as a natural insect repellant. You can wear it in a tincture, dab it on a regular candle, or sprinkle the fresh herb around your dining area.

To make your own bug spray start with about 6 ounces of fresh, clean basil leaves (preferably ones that have not been treated in any way). Steep them in 4 ounces of boiling water until they turn translucent. Cool and squeeze, retaining the liquid. Add 4 ounces of clear alcohol to the basil water and transfer it into a spray bottle for easy application.

Food Selection, Preparation and Precooking

The way you shop, prepare and precook your barbecue ties into food safety guidelines that help decrease the risk of foodborne illness. You'll get to read more about this topic in upcoming chapters, but for now let's build a foundation, starting with your trip to the market. Always leave refrigerator items for the last part of your shopping trip. Set them in your cart in such a way that raw meat packages do not touch your other ingredients. These should also get packed separately to prevent **cross-contamination**.

Shop Talk...

Cross-Contamination; N. Cross-contamination happens when a food containing micro-organisms like bacteria come into contact with other ingredients that lack them. This transfers the bacteria to the other part of your meal that won't get cooked. Raw meat is a chief offender, which is why it's important to clean cutting boards, your hands, and countertops after initial prep work with it.

WARNING!

Refrigerated food left out more than 2 hours isn't safe to eat. Ground meats that you don't plan to use within the next two days should go directly to your freezer. Other cuts can remain in the refrigerator for about 4 days before freezing without risk.

On the Dial: Defrosting

Frozen items require defrosting before you can cook them. The easiest defrosting method is putting the food into your refrigerator until it thaws. While a microwave defrosts quickly, it can also start pre-cooking your food if not monitored carefully. This creates a less desirable (and sometimes tougher) finished product. Only use the microwave for items that will go directly on your pre-heated grill afterward.

Majestic Marinades and Righteous Rubs

Marinades and rubs give your meal an extra layer of flavor, and they also tenderize the food. The USDA recommends that both marinades and rubs work their magic in the safety of a container in the refrigerator. If you plan on using either as part of your grilling sauce or spices, put a portion aside before you apply it to the food. Alternatively, pour off the marinade when your food is ready for grilling and bring it to a full rolling boil. This should kill any potential bacteria from raw meat.

BARBECUE to Go

The Picnic Basket

A lot of barbecue plans include taking food to another location. There is a very simple cooking mantra for you to remember not only for your grilled food, but all culinary endeavors: Keep cold food cold and hot food hot. Yes, I know that sounds like "common sense" but when you consider that over 50 million Americans get

continued...

food poisoning annually, it appears my mother was right when she said, "common sense isn't common." 50 million equates to 1 in 6 Americans getting sick from improperly prepared or stored food. Either food safety messages aren't reaching everyone, or people don't take them seriously.

Use ice packs in a good cooler so water doesn't seep into your creation, and remember to cover meats with a food storage bag so they do not touch other elements of your recipe. If you have a vacuum sealer, that's even better. The prime temperature for transporting cold food is 37 degrees F. Keep hot food above the temperature of 140 degrees F.

WARNING!

Between 40 and 140 degrees F, bacteria begins to grow very quickl—in just 20 minutes, the amount of bacteria in a piece of food can double. That's why this temperature range is called the Danger Zone. Never leave food at room temperature for more than 2 hours. When the heat outside reaches 90 degrees F, put food into a suitable cooler or refrigerator after 1 hour.

Pack your cooler at the last minute, moving items from the freezer or refrigerator directly onto the ice. Put the cooler in a shaded area with good ventilation. Don't unpack your cooler until you're actually ready for grilling.

Tips: Just Chillin' Cooler Tips

♦ Block ice lasts longer than ice cubes.

♦ Use recycled, clean milk or pop containers filled with water as alternatives to block or cube ice (this keeps water from leaking into your food).

♦ Think about the timing for your recipe and meal. Put the last items you plan to use at the bottom of your cooler. Continue layering chronologically ending with the first items for your meal on top.

♦ Don't pack too tightly. Leave a little air space between items, which actually slows ice melt and helps maintain a consistent internal temperature throughout the cooler.

♦ Packing your picnic blanket or other cloth items around the cooler in your car actually provides insulation (avoid putting the cooler in the trunk as that part of the car gets very hot).

Use proper defrosting, marinating and cooler packing methods that keep your food safe from bacteria.

Tips

♦ Put your marinade into a vacuum sealer bag with the food. This way it continues soaking up goodness until you're ready to cook.

♦ If you do not have ice packs use a cake pan or other flat pan for freezing sheets of ice. Put those in the cooler with aluminum foil overtop to deter wetness.

♦ If you're bringing beverage bottles you can freeze them and use them as a cold source, particularly for lunches and small items.

Beverages are more easily managed, but make sure you have a ready supply of ice. Hint: try having a separate cooler just for carrying your cooling component, and refill your main cooler from there.

Huddle 'Round The Campfire

Barbecue often shows up at camping events too. Short hikes are one thing, but food sitting in coolers for days at varying temperatures can become a recipe for food poisoning. You don't have to give up grilling altogether just to enjoy the great outdoors, however. This is where carefully planned food preparation and storage become even more vital.

When you're camping the rule of keeping cold things cold certainly applies. Keeping hot things hot might be trickier unless you intend to keep an attended fire

continued...

burning throughout the day. That's why I recommend pre-cooking and freezing your meals, packing the one that you intend to use last at the bottom of the cooler, and the first one on top. That way you aren't constantly moving food in and out of your cooler (this is also a very rustic version of *mise en place*!) Remember—double wrap or seal everything to prevent cross-contamination.

WARNING!

Always check to see if your campsite offers clean water. If it does not, make sure you bring enough for drinking and for keeping your barbecue tools, plates, and grill clean throughout your stay. Remember to diligently wash your hands after touching meat before touching anything else in your recipe.

Now, just because you're getting cozy with Mother Nature doesn't mean foregoing all your modern conveniences. Take your food thermometer with you. This way you can double check the internal temperatures of the food. Cook ground beef, pork, and lamb to 160 degrees F, pork or lamb chops and roasts require at least 145 degrees, and poultry should reach 165 degrees on the thermometer. Read the instructions provided on the unit, as different thermometers require different placement in the meat for accurate readings.

Food Safety History

Special Feature…

We have come a long way from when Caveman Og tossed food on a fire and hoped for the best. Abraham Lincoln created the USDA Division of Chemistry in 1862. In 1883 a Doctor named W. Wiley became chief of this division and began raising public awareness about foodborne illness. Eventually he became the driving force behind the Pure Food and Drugs Act. One year later, the USDA Bureau of Animal Industry began regulating diseased animals; their key charge was keeping them out of human consumption.

Remain aware and mindful of food temperatures both when cooking and storing them. When in doubt, check the USDA Guidelines for safe grilling.

Tailgate Grilling

Ready to take your new barbecue know-how to the next game? You can, but as with other locations for grilling there are some guidelines that you need to follow. Since your average parking lot doesn't have clean water, you'll have to carry your own. You can also pack some antiseptic wipes that you can use on grilling surfaces or your hands when moving from one type of food to another.

Just as with camping, you need a good cooler that keeps your food cold. Follow the same guidelines for wrapping and separating the items as before—double wrap or vacuum seal and keep raw meat away from other food. Note that it's not recommended that you partially cook your food before the tailgate party. Either cook it fully and warm it up, or start from raw. The in-between stage acts as a breeding ground for bacteria.

Tips

♦ Don't pack your cooler too soon before the game. You need to maintain a temperature of 40° F or below from home until you get set up and start grilling.

♦ You can use an appliance thermometer inside the cooler to check temperature levels. Avoid opening the cooler more often than necessary, as that allows heat in.

♦ If you're transporting a hot plate it must be consumed within two hours for safety. Otherwise you'll have to rewarm it to 165 degrees F.

From Grill to Table and Beyond

Serving food is another area where bacteria can come into play. Never put a finished dish on a plate that previously had raw poultry or meat unless it's been properly cleaned. When temperatures reach over 90 degrees F°, make sure your serving platters don't stay out for over 1 hour. At that time, package things up using air-tight food storage containers and return them to a cool environment.

Once you're home check your cooler's temperature again. If it remained under 40 degrees F°, you'll have some delectable leftovers for another day (provided there was anything left!)

Author's Aside

I have learned that you do not need to cook all elements or servings at a barbecue to have a successful gathering. In fact, by cooking only what you need when you need it, you're making a safer meal.

THE TAKEAWAY

▶ Safety first: When in doubt—throw it out.

▶ Good planning and preparation creates a much more relaxed atmosphere whether you're cooking for family or a whole slew of guests.

▶ Temperature affects food safety both in the way you store an item and the internal temperature to which you cook each component.

▶ Proper methods for defrosting, marinating, and packing your barbecue ingredients on ice help keep the food safe from bacteria.

▶ Cook smaller portions based on the order of your meal. You can pay closer attention to the food and keep the remaining portions chilling until you need them.

*"I love grilling. Grilling is an incredible way to keep healthy.
And you can marinate both with a dry rub and also wet marinades.
You can marinate juniper berry or a little bit of olive oil and some
citrus and fresh herbs—all of that sort of stuff."*

—Curtis Stone, celebrity chef

5

Marvelous Marinades & Rubs

Fun With Flavor

Now we start building your flavor profiles. If you do a lot of cooking in your kitchen, this won't be difficult for you to master. You're just transferring the concepts into marinades and barbecue rub. However, I recognize that not everyone who wants to barbecue also cooks regularly, so you may need a little seasoning savvy. Read on!

There will be lots of examples of marinades and rubs in this chapter that you can whip up depending on what you're cooking. However, there's one important factor: what's in your pantry today? If you don't want to buy a ton of new herbs and spices (which gets costly very quickly), then you may want to work with what you have already. The key is finding recipes that utilize your on-hand inventory.

Special Feature...

Common Culinary Herbs & Spices

Certain herbs and spices are used more often in the kitchen. Some of these are baking spices, but don't let that limit you. Sweet and savory both have roles in barbecue marinades and rubs.

Sweet(ish) spices are comprised of cinnamon, nutmeg, ginger, vanilla bean, and allspice. Savory-sweet herbs include basil, cumin, paprika, sage, saffron, and thyme. Savory ingredients are things like bay, red pepper flakes, chili powder, cloves, dill, garlic, onion, oregano, salt, pepper, rosemary, and tarragon.

Don't sweat it if you haven't got them all. Buy small initially until you see what you use regularly. Keep dried herbs in a cool, dark location for longevity. Fresh herbs last longer in the refrigerator.

When you can't smell a dry spice upon opening, it's past its expiration and functionality.

Store Bought or Fresh?

The alternative to using what you have available is buying one or two barbecue blends at the supermarket that match your planned menus. There are numerous producers of specialty barbecue items. Many stores carry McCormic Grillmates. They're tasty and not terribly expensive. Simply Organic is another good selection. If you're not sure, try checking with some grilling friends to see what they prefer (and, hey, ask for a taste test!).

Author's Aside

If you're looking for mix-n-match or premade dry blends in a variety of sizes, my go-to store online is SpiceBarn.com. For sauces, marinades and condiments I often find great deals at Farawayfoods.com. I have ordered from both companies for many years now and never experienced any problems with variety, delivery, or quality.

Quality herbs and spices are the backbone of good marinades and barbecue rubs. When you can use fresh ingredients, do so. Just remember you'll need three times as much fresh ingredients in a recipe that calls for dry herbs or spices. Always add spices slowly so that you can adjust for personal tastes.

Another choice is indulging in the wonderful world of fresh herbs and spices. While dried or frozen herbs and spices last longer, most chefs, including me, agree that "fresher is better." It's just that the amount used for the recipe changes. The ratio I recommend is 3 times the amount of fresh herb to 1 part dry (the dry components being more concentrated).

TIP Less is more. Always start out slowly with your seasoning, tasting as you go. Everyone's palate is different. You can always add more spice, but you can never take it back. Also keep a list of the herbs in a recipe and put it out where guests can see it. This avoids problems with food allergies.

The All-Purpose Palate Pleasure

It's nice to have at least one marinade and barbecue rub that's all-purpose. From that basic foundation you can build anything, but if you just want quick and easy there's no reason to fuss further.

One of the most common "everything" marinades is plain old Italian salad dressing. For broad application I suggest a zesty oil-based brand. However, the creamy style Italian works as an interesting variation, particularly with chicken and vegetables (I see kabobs in your future).

If you'd like to make your own oil-based dressing it's not difficult. Begin with 1 Tb. each of parsley flakes, garlic powder, and onion powder. Add 2 Tbsp. oregano flakes, 1 tsp. each black pepper, basil and **kosher** salt, and ¼ tsp each thyme and celery salt. Mix and transfer to a labeled air-tight container until you need to mix up the marinade.

Shop Talk...

> **Kosher Salt**; N. Kosher salt has larger grains than table salt. It also is free of additives like Iodine.

To create liquid marinade begin with 2 Tbsp. of dry mix to ¼ cup white vinegar, 2/3 cup **extra virgin olive oil**, and 2 Tbsp. water. Whisk thoroughly. This makes one cup. Note that you can use this Italian blend as a serviceable rub too. Just apply it dry to any meat, poultry, or seafood and let them sit in the refrigerator for about an hour before grilling. You can eliminate the salt if you wish and for more heat, substitute red pepper flakes.

Shop Talk...

> **Extra Virgin Olive Oil**; N. Extra Virgin Olive Oil is considered the highest quality of olive oil available. It is free of acid and made without additives. The International Olive Counsel has a trained panel that checks olive oil in order to award it this designation. Depending on the types of olives and the manufacturer, Extra Virgin Olive oil may taste slightly peppery, bitter, or fruity.

By the way, this mix is perfectly pleasing on salads. It can also be used as a culinary baste or exterior spice in the oven.

KEY POINT *The herbs and spices used in barbecue rubs can easily become part of a marinade and the dry ingredients in a marinade can transform into the foundation for a rub.*

Meat Matters:

Beef, Chicken and Pork

Beef Blends

Different types of beef have different types of natural flavor. You want to coax that flavor out without completely covering it up with your marinade or barbecue rub. To give you an example, beef ribs accept a wide variety of flavors and handle lavish amounts of components, including ginger, chives, savory, celery, oregano, and basil, just to name a few. By comparison a lovely filet requires a frugal use of spices (I suggest no more than three—parsley, rosemary, and thyme) so it can really shine.

The most common herbs paired with beef include:

- ♦ Basil
- ♦ Bay
- ♦ Chive (*or onion powder*)
- ♦ Cilantro
- ♦ Garlic
- ♦ Ginger

- ♦ Paprika (*plain or smoky*)
- ♦ Horseradish
- ♦ Rosemary
- ♦ Tarragon
- ♦ Thyme
- ♦ Salt & Pepper

Special Feature...

Signature Salts

Most households have table salt. Some also have Kosher salt, but did you know there is a whole world of gourmet salts that you can use in barbecue? Fleur de Sel from France has a delicate, mineral rich flavor that is good for that final touch before serving. Gray salt has a much stronger mineral taste best on hearty foods. Smoked salt, as the name implies, imparts a smoky flavor to barbecue without having to use wood chips. Hawaiian red salt is a beautiful large-grained salt that adds depth to vegetables and fish, and Japanese Shio salt provides background flavor that won't overwhelm your dish.

To make a beef marinade you begin with a liquid. What liquid depends on what tastes you're hoping to achieve. For example, if you want an Asian style beef you might use soy sauce, rice vinegar, ginger, and chives (and perhaps even a little **five spice** just for a twist).

Shop Talk...

Five Spice Powder; This blend, common to Chinese and Asian cooking has five spices as the name implies. It may not, however, always have the same five spices from brand to brand. Common ingredients used for Five Spice include cloves, fennel, star anise, cinnamon, Sichuan pepper, ginger, turmeric, nutmeg, licorice, orange, and black pepper. For beef, it's most effective on fatty cuts.

A blend we like around our house starts with a beer or wine base and incorporates garlic, ginger, and pepper (note: if you don't like beer or wine you can substitute orange juice).

Other options include:

- ▶ Red wine vinegar, brown sugar, Worcestershire sauce, ketchup, onion powder, and red pepper flakes
- ▶ Olive oil, soy sauce, lemon juice, parsley, basil, garlic, and black pepper
- ▶ Beer, honey mustard, lemon rind, garlic, salt, and pepper
- ▶ Red wine, cumin, coriander, onion powder, garlic powder, and sea salt
- ▶ Red wine vinegar, cilantro, garlic, lime juice, olive oil, and cumin

TIP In choosing red wine or beer for marinade I strongly advocate one that you would actually drink. Take a taste of a cooking wine you get at the supermarket—BLECH. If you wouldn't drink it, why would you want to use it for flavoring your food?

So what about beef barbecue rubs? You can leave out the wet component in any of the example blends and you'll have a serviceable rub. Here are some other ideas to get your creative juices flowing:

- ▶ Chili powder, smoky paprika, mustard powder, cumin, coriander, cracked pepper, and coarse salt
- ▶ Paprika, garlic, onion, brown sugar, red pepper flakes, salt, and pepper
- ▶ Celery seed, onion powder, oregano, thyme, mustard, coriander, allspice, and brown sugar
- ▶ Chipotle pepper, orange rind, onion powder, and Worcestershire powder

TIP There are companies that specialize in dehydrated herbs, spices, and even fruits. This gives you more options in making your dry rubs. You can find examples on websites like **www.nuts.com** and **www.americanspice.com**

You've probably noticed by now that I'm not giving you proportions in these suggestions. There are two reasons. First, there are specific recipes later in this book that provide measurements. You can use those recipes and mix them up by substituting or adding some of your favorite flavors. If you get stuck on one framework it's less likely that you'll experiment and find your own specialty blends. Secondly, everyone's tastes are different. Some like it hot, some like it sweet, some prefer simple and savory.

The key to success in making your marinades and rubs is to start out small and build from there. In general, use powerful spices like rosemary sparingly, so that all your herbs and spices have a chance to shine.

 *Just because this is **Grilling for Beginners** doesn't mean you can't experiment. In fact, that's one of the important aspects to your learning process. While you may have a few blends fall flat along the way, if you're tasting as you go you won't ruin your whole meal.*

Fixin' Chicken

Unless you're vegetarian or vegan, it's really hard to imagine barbecue without talking about chicken. The National Chicken Counsel tells us that at the Super Bowl of 2014 alone over 1.2 billion (that's with a b, folks) chicken wings were consumed. Now start thinking about all those chicken barbecue fundraisers you see, let alone the friends, co-workers, and total strangers who grill up chicken every day. In my opinion, chicken is the king of the grilling coop. There's a good reason for its popularity – chicken accepts flavor very well, especially when it's parboiled or skinless. Chicken can take deep-down flavoring too, especially if you use an **injector**.

Shop Talk...

Flavor Injector: N. This is a nifty kitchen gadget that people use frequently for turkey but also large piece (or whole) chickens. You fill it with wine, sauce, butter, juice, or sauces and spices, then insert it into the meat in various places. This brings rich flavors to all of your meat, not just the surface. These are not expensive, and they function on vegetables, fruit and other meat too!

Common herbs and spices paired with chicken include:

- ◆ Coriander
- ◆ Lemon
- ◆ Garlic
- ◆ Parsley
- ◆ Marjoram
- ◆ Dill

- ◆ Sage
- ◆ Rosemary
- ◆ Thyme
- ◆ Ginger
- ◆ Tarragon
- ◆ Basil

There are also some blends that you can find at most international supermarkets like the Indian blend Garam Masala (cumin, coriander, cloves, nutmeg, cinnamon, cardamom, and pepper), the Jamaican Jerk blend (allspice, hot peppers, cloves, cinnamon, nutmeg, thyme, garlic, scallion or onion, and salt), and the French Herbes de Provence (oregano, savory, marjoram, rosemary, thyme, and lavender).

For your marinade, common bases include lemon or lime juice, soy sauce, beer, and white wine. Here are some marinade blend ideas:

- ► **Balsamic vinegar, oregano, rosemary, whole mustard seed, olive oil, salt, and pepper**
- ► **Canola oil, parsley, Worcestershire, white wine, lemon juice, and garlic**
- ► **Pineapple juice, honey, ginger, soy sauce, garlic powder, and onion powder**
- ► **Raspberry or strawberry juice, rice wine, flaked red pepper, rice vinegar, and coconut oil**
- ► **Lemon juice, brown sugar, cracked peppercorns, dill, or basil**
- ► **White wine, orange marmalade, fresh green onions, and malt vinegar**

TIP Some grillers do a hybrid form of rub that has a thick or semi-creamy wet component. A good example is a mustard rub using honey mustard with onion, garlic, and parsley mixed in. While this is not a dry rub per se, it sticks to the meat where dry spices sometimes flake off. It also creates a tasty crust.

So how about some barbecue rubs? To be honest, you can use nearly anything on chicken (or poultry) and have it taste good. Poultry seasoning comes to mind immediately (sage, marjoram, thyme, rosemary, nutmeg, and pepper). But you probably want to add more layers of flavor. Here are some examples:

▶ Honey powder, paprika, mustard powder, onion powder, garlic powder, salt, and pepper

▶ Brown sugar, chili powder, cayenne, garlic powder, onion powder, salt, and pepper

▶ Worcestershire powder, basil, oregano, garlic powder, onion powder, and cracked pepper

▶ Chili powder, cumin, taco seasoning, lemon zest, vinegar powder, and sugar

Remember that fruits pair wonderfully with chicken so you can also use orange rind, grapefruit rind, apple peel etc., as part of your rub.

Special Feature...

Flower Power

The art of cooking with flowers is experiencing a renaissance. There are a lot of petals that are not only tasty but good for you. For pairing with chicken, lavender and rose work great. Other flowers you can bring to your table include Calendula, Carnation, Chrysanthemum, Dandelion, Day Lily, Honeysuckle, Nasturtium, Red clove, Squash blossom, and Violet. Add them to greens for a whimsical spring or summer salad.

Chicken is perhaps the most adaptable of meats when it comes to accepting barbecue flavors. You really can't go wrong. Remember to try new flavors like mixing fruit or flowers into your recipe. Both provide aromatic notes too!

Pork Pairings

Ah, it's time for ribs! I confess it took me nearly 30 years to perfect ribs. Pork is challenging because it is so easy to dry the meat out. So with any pork product, low and slow is very good. You can watch it carefully that way. I often pre-cook pork in the oven and finish it on the grill for this very reason. Look for a half-way point (about 74 degrees internal temperature). While that's coming up, prep the grill so the meat goes directly from one heat source to another.

Traditional herbs and spice for pork include:

- ♦ Herbes de Provence
- ♦ Marjoram
- ♦ Basil
- ♦ Thyme
- ♦ Garlic

- ♦ Savory
- ♦ Fennel
- ♦ Oregano
- ♦ Rosemary
- ♦ Ginger

This looks strikingly similar to chicken with good reason. Cooking with pork is like painting on a blank wall. It's not as absorbent as chicken but still accepts flavor readily. Here are some blends for your enjoyment:

- ► Olive oil, soy sauce, Worchestershire sauce, red or white vinegar, lemon, salt, pepper, and parsley
- ► Pineapple juice and crushed pineapple, soy sauce, honey, rice vinegar, ginger, and cloves
- ► *Sake*, brown sugar, and chili peppers
- ► Vegetable oil, cider vinegar, minced onion, and hot or sweet pepper
- ► Peanut oil, Worchestershire or soy, balsamic vinegar, minced tomato, and liquid smoke
- ► Bourbon, brown sugar or honey, minced orange, and stone ground mustard

Author's Aside

One of our favorite sandwiches begins with thin sliced grilled pork, a slice of barbecued bourbon pineapple, lettuce, and a hard roll. Add whatever condiments you like. Fast, easy and incredibly tasty. You can substitute an orange or apple slice if you're not a fan of pineapple.

Shop Talk...

Sake: N. A fermented beverage made from rice that comes from Japan. The process of making it is similar to beer, but sake has a far higher alcohol content. By comparison, beer averages 5%, whereas sake goes up to 20%.

Now for some barbecued pork rubs:

- ► Garlic, chili powder, brown sugar, paprika, salt, and cracked pepper
- ► Cumin, cayenne, hawaiian sugar, chili powder, black pepper, and kosher salt
- ► Smoky paprika, garlic, chipotle, onion powder, celery salt, brown sugar, thyme, oregano, mustard, and allspice
- ► Paprika, garlic, sugar, mustard, ginger, orange or lemon zest, salt, and pepper
- ► White sugar, paprika, ginger, ground onion, rosemary, and pepper

Paprika

While it may not taste like it, paprika actually comes from chili peppers. It was popularized in Hungary, Spain, and Portugal. The Spanish version was (and still is) typically smoked, adding greater depth. Until the 1920s most paprika was piquant, until a botanist created a milder plant that also had a hint of sweetness. Cooks use this spice not only for flavoring but for adding color, which is why it appears in so many barbecue recipes.

KEY POINT *Paprika is one of the most widely used spices for barbecue rubs because it adds great color without overwhelming the taste of the rest of your blend.*

By Land or By Sea

Meat isn't the only thing you'll find on barbecue grills around the world. There's also fish, shellfish, and vegetables, all of which can be a little tricky. Delicate fishes like tilapia, and shellfish like shrimp, can actually begin cooking when you put them in a marinade or use a rub. This is particularly true when using an acid like lime or lemon. In fact, certain types of culinary methods take advantage of that including **ceviche or poke**.

ShopTalk...

Ceviche; N: A dish common to coastal towns, particularly in the Southern U.S. and Mexico, that utilizes raw fish that's pre-cured in lemon, lime, or orange juice, hot pepper and other regional spice blends.

Poke; N: A Hawaiian dish made from Ahi tuna that's marinated with soy, sea salt, sesame oil, and hot pepper. Some versions include seaweed, roe, or tomato.

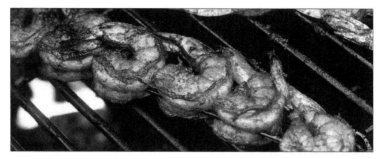

Fish & Shellfish Flavors

Some grillers get leery about cooking with fish because it often sticks to the grill. There is a simple secret however. Just remember to treat your grill grates with oil and let one side sear. If the fish isn't releasing from the surface, it's not seared yet and will fall apart. Also, while denser fish like salmon take to grilling relatively easily, you can use a wire mesh basket for delicate cuts (note treat that with oil too!). With a one inch piece of fish you need to cook it for about 4 minutes per side for doneness.

Here is a list of herbs that frequently show up in fish and shellfish recipes:

- ◆ Allspice
- ◆ Bay
- ◆ Cardamom
- ◆ Chili powder
- ◆ Cilantro
- ◆ Coriander
- ◆ Dill
- ◆ Mustard
- ◆ Oregano
- ◆ Paprika
- ◆ Sesame

- ◆ Anise
- ◆ Basil
- ◆ Cayenne
- ◆ Chives
- ◆ Cinnamon
- ◆ Curry
- ◆ Garlic
- ◆ **Old Bay**
- ◆ Pepper
- ◆ Saffron
- ◆ Citrus

Remember when combining spices and a liquid base for marinating seafood that any acid contributes to pre-cooking. This sometimes results in toughness, so remember that seafood recipes shouldn't marinate as long as beef or poultry.

Shop Talk...

Old Bay; N: This herb blend marketed by McCormick appeared in 1939 in the Chesapeake Bay area. It integrates a mixture of paprika, celery salt, mustard, red pepper, cloves, nutmeg, ginger, cardamom, allspice, and mace, and is used predominantly for seasoning shrimp and crab.

Here are some blends to get you started:

▶ **White wine, orange zest, honey, ginger, and red pepper flakes**
▶ **Bourbon, soy sauce, garlic, and pineapple**
▶ **Cider vinegar, mustard, Worcestershire, chili pepper, sugar, and onion**
▶ **Sea salt, white pepper, lemon juice, olive oil, and parsley**
▶ **Lime juice, tequila, cilantro, and salt**
▶ **Beer, orange juice, oregano, thyme, basil, and powdered mustard**

As for rubs, tinker with these ideas:

▶ **Garlic powder, rosemary, cayenne, sweet paprika, salt, and black pepper**
▶ **Chipotle, white pepper, oregano, thyme, and paprika**
▶ **Sea salt, coriander, chili powder, smoked paprika, thyme, and black pepper**
▶ **Lemon zest, orange zest, onion powder, garlic, and cilantro**

Many of the blends used for chicken work effectively on fish too. Just remember that many types of fish are more delicate than pork, so use a lighter hand with your flavorings.

Vegetables

Vegetables play a role in barbecue marinades and rubs in one of two ways. First is as part of the marinade or rub itself. I like to do this particularly with kabobs so that all the flavors marry together. Alternatively you may grill the vegetables and use marinade and rub for another layer of flavor (in some cases, you can do both!). Some of the vegetables that best accept marinade and rub flavors include squash, zucchini, mushrooms, tomatoes, and broccoli.

There are a ton of herbs and spices that match vegetables. A lot here depends on what you're grilling. Leeks, for example, taste good with dill, bay, celery salt and/or mustard, while eggplant benefits from garlic, parsley, oregano, mint, rosemary, and basil. For this reason, I suggest consulting your recipe or doing a fast search online regarding the vegetables you plan to use. There are numerous websites where you can find excellent ideas and information—you can find my recommendations in the Deep Dish at the end of this book.

Soft vegetables accept marinade and flavoring more readily than harder produce like potatoes and carrots. However, sliced or diced hard vegetables can bring an extra layer of taste to a marinade.

Here are some vegetable marinade blends for you to try:

- **Extra virgin olive oil, soy sauce, garlic, onion (fresh or powder), and lemon juice**
- **Pineapple juice, Dijon mustard, vegetable oil, maple syrup, white vinegar, and pepper**
- **All-purpose marinade**
- **Orange marmalade, olive oil, malt vinegar, and red chili flakes,**
- **Soy sauce, rice vinegar, ginger, and sesame oil**

As far as rubs, you don't so much "rub" a vegetable as sprinkle it with whatever blend you make. You can do this while you cook the dish. This has the extra advantage of replacing any spice or marinade that falls off during grilling.

 For intense vegetable flavor, add a packet of dehydrated vegetable soup mix to your marinade or grind it up fine and sprinkle it on the vegetables as they cook.

THE TAKEAWAY

- ▶ Use the best fresh or dried spices you can find for your marinades and rubs. Remember to add them slowly, tasting as you go.

- ▶ The herbs in commercial or homemade rubs can easily transform into a marinade simply by adding a liquid base.

- ▶ Experimentation is part of the learning process. Write down your successes for future reference.

- ▶ For flexibility work with chicken.

- ▶ Paprika is the most common spice used in barbecue rubs

- ▶ Many of the spice blends for chicken work well on fish too.

- ▶ Soft vegetables accept flavor from marinade, but harder vegetables or vegetable powder can go into your blend for greater flavor.

"When I want to kick it up, I like to add hardwood chips
or chunks to the grill; it adds bold smoky flavors."

—Emeril Lagasse, celebrity chef & restaurateur

6

Smoking Hot Ideas

Where There's Smoke, There's Flavor

The aroma and flavor of smoke gives your barbecue endeavors a whole new dimension in flavor. Between the smoke of wood and the drippings from your main dish, you'll create a nearly irresistible scent that will coax even a slumbering grandfather to come take a peek. So what are the great secrets of smoking for the most tantalizing results?

First, bear in mind that if you want to smoke using a gas grill, you're likely going to need a special attachment in which your smoking wood resides. There are other ways to coax smoke out of a gas grill, but we will talk about that later. For this reason, my beginner barbecue buffs that chose charcoal grills have a foundation on which to place the wood and get it up to heat relatively quickly.

The Invention of Charcoal

In 1897 Ellsworth Zwoyer patented the charcoal briquette design in Pennsylvania. He went on to building processing plants after World War One, one of which was in Buffalo, NY. Later, Henry Ford and Thomas Edison built on Zwoyer's idea, creating a wood-scrap based briquette that would eventually become the property of E.G. Kingsford for commercial marketing.

Another element smoking adds to your food (specifically meat products) is the elusive "**smoke ring**." Watch any heavy duty smoking competition and the contestants seem to seek this Holy Grail of Grilling with a passion rivalling King Arthur!

Shop Talk...

Smoke Ring; N. A pink layer beneath the surface of barbecued meat. This forms when nitric acid produced by the burning wood mixes with moisture in the smoking unit mix, then gets absorbed by your main dish.

The smoke ring alone isn't enough reason to say "I do." Most experts agree it doesn't alter the flavor and you can still end up with a dry piece of meat that has an attractive ring. A ¼" ring, however, is often a telltale visual sign of a skilled cooking process that should be tasty. As the old saying goes, we eat with our eyes, and there's an aesthetically pleasing appeal to the way the smoke ring looks.

The key is not getting so hung up on creating a fanciful ring that you forget all about taking proper care of your food throughout the smoking process. This includes monitoring temperature in the smoker, in your meat, and adding whatever other mops or sauces the recipe calls for at the proper intervals.

Author's Aside

*Some people avoid using mops or sauces for the initial several hours of smoking so that the flavors don't fight with each other, and the meat can accept the smoke more readily. There are varying opinions on this, but my best results have been those that use a **brine** or marinade followed by smoke, and finished with a mop or sauce (if desired).*

Shop Talk...

Brine; N. Brining is an alternative to marinade. It employs salt, a liquid (usually water), and spices in the average proportion of 1 gallon liquid to 1 cup of salt mixed together. The amount of time the brine needs in order to work depends on the size of your main dish. A whole turkey can take about 38 hours to properly carry the salt-liquid-herb mixture into the meat, but it results in a very moist, flavor-enhanced dish.

Mops and brines work very well in smoking. They help the smoke "cling" to the meat while also imparting subtle flavor. This also keeps the meat moist.

Wood and Wisdom

There is an old aphorism that says where there's smoke, there's fire. As it turns out, where there's smoke, there's wood! The first thing you need to know is that not all wood is created equal. In fact, smoking wood isn't even uniform in size and shape. You'll find that barbecue aficionados eventually gravitate to one or two varieties of wood depending on the size and shape of their equipment. So what's best for you?

Measuring Up Wood

Determining your favorite smoking wood is partially experimentation and partially a little knowledge of what's what.

Let's start with chunk wood. These are roughly the size of a small fist. The advantage to chunk wood is that it's slow-burning, meaning you don't have to restock it so often. This, in turn, keeps heat inside your unit. That advantage makes chunks among the most popular choices with grillers.

For larger units, hardwood logs are another option. The key to using logs effectively is pre-burning them until they reach a good smoking temperature for their size (around 250 degrees F). Logs are a little harder to manage, but like chunk wood you don't have to open your unit as frequently to keep the wood stocked.

Chips are another option. You can buy these nearly anywhere. They catch fire quickly but also burn out quickly. That makes them best for recipes with short cooking times. Food-grade pellets also provide fast smokiness. Add them to the fire during the last 20 minutes of cooking. In both cases, a good size handful or two should obtain the desired results.

TIP In shopping around for smoking wood you may come across something called pellet bricks. These are similar to pellets (made from compressed sawdust) but act like chunk wood. They are a suitable alternative to chunks, providing you with low moisture, good heat, smoke, and longevity.

Read pellet and brick labels carefully. Buy only FOOD GRADE brands. Other types of pellets are typically for heaters and contain additives that will ruin the flavor of your food.

WARNING!

KEY POINT

Always use food-grade wood for smoking. Chunk wood is an excellent choice for extended cooking, while chips help get your smoker fired up more quickly.

A Walk in the Woods

When you look at various types of smoking woods, you might shrug and think: *They look the same to me.*

Many woods do look similar to each other, but the flavors vary dramatically.

Generally speaking, smoking woods come in one of three categories:

Mild, Medium, and Hardy.

Mild woods include those from fruit trees—they are perfect for delicate components like white fish. Medium wood is more distinctive but won't overwhelm your recipes' flavors. These include hickory and oak, both of which go nicely with beef and pork. Finally, your hardy woods are those like mesquite, which is best used on cuts that can handle the intense flavor (Texas-style brisket, for example).

The Marriage Between Wood and Recipe

Your smoking wood choice matters to the entire union of flavors you're creating. So then, what types of wood pair with specific foods? Let's take a look!

Wood:	Category:	Pairs With:	Flavor:
Acacia	Medium	Beef & Vegetables	Like mesquite
Alder	Mild	Beef, Fish & Pork	Subtle
Almond	Medium	All Meat	Nutty
Apple	Mild	Chicken, Pork Fruit & Carrots	Demure
Ash	Medium	Red Meat & Fish	Smokey
Bay	Mild to Medium	Vegetables & Meat	Spicy
Birch	Mild to Medium	Pork & Poultry	Like Maple
Blackberry	Mild	Game Birds	Slightly Sweet
Butternut	Hardy	Game Meats	Strong Smoke
Cherry	Mild	Beef, Fish, Chicken, Pork, Fruit & Onion	Slightly Sweet
Chestnut	Mild	Most Meat, Fruit & Vegetables	Sweet-Nutty
Cottonwood	Very Mild	Delicate Meat, Fish, Fruit & Vegetables	Like Alder
Grapevine	Hardy	Red Meat & Game Meat	Tart-Fruity
Guava	Mild	Beef, Lamb, Poultry & Fish	Lightly Sweet
Hickory	Medium to Strong	Poultry & Vegetables	Robust
Lemon	Medium	Beef, Pork & Poultry	Fruity

Use aggressive woods like Mesquite with equally aggressive meats that have a strong flavor, such as game meat.

Wood:	Category:	Pairs With:	Flavor:
Lilac	Mild	Pork, Poultry & Cheese	Flowery
Maple	Mild to Medium	Pork, Poultry & Fruit	Honeyed
Mesquite	Hardy	Beef, Pork, Poultry, Fish & Hard Vegetables	Strong
Mulberry	Mild	Ham, Poultry & Beef	Tangy
Oak	Medium	Beef, Pork, Hen Red Meat & Fish	Nutty
Orange	Medium	Beef, Pork, Poultry & Some Fish	Mild Fruity
Peach	Mild	Fish, Turkey & Pork	Sweet, Woody
Pecan	Medium to Strong	Beef, Chicken & Pork	Spicy
Pimento	Mild to Medium	Chicken & Fish	Peppery
Wine Barrels	Medium	Beef, Pork, Fruit & Vegetables	Like Oak

Barking Up the Wrong Tree?

After reading this list, you might wonder if there are any types of wood that you should NOT use for smoking food. The answer is yes. In fact there are several rules to choosing suitable smoking woods. There are various bushes and trees that naturally carry toxins that are harmful to humans. First, avoid any soft wood or gum trees like pines, fir, elderberry, and sycamore. The sap creates funny flavors and may give some people allergic reactions. Second, don't go dumpster diving for your smoking wood. No lumber yard scraps, no stained wood, no furniture remainders, no old pallets. All of these may have been treated with chemicals that your food absorbs. Similar to safe food handling guidelines—if you're not sure what you have, throw it out.

Finally, even with safe wood, avoid any pieces that show signs of fungus, mold, or rot.

Smoking Without a Smoker

Not everyone can afford a grilling unit that has a smoker or a separate smoking unit. So how do you get that great smoky flavor without special equipment? Well, if you're using charcoal there's no problem—just sprinkle wood chips over the top of the charcoal once it's heated properly. Gas grills are a little bit more difficult.

What we did prior to having a smoker was simply make a little aluminum foil holder for wood chips or chunks. Think of it like making an Origami box. Take a piece of foil and fold over the edges 3 times so that they're sturdy. Next, bend those edges upward so you have a firm edge and flat bottom. Poke some holes in the bottom with a toothpick for air circulation. Fill that with your chips and place them over a high gas flame. It will take a little longer to get them smoking because of the foil layer but it does work. Once they start smoking, reduce your heat level to about 225° F for a low-slow smoke.

Alternatively, you can purchase an aluminum bread or loaf pan and use that. They're inexpensive and easy. In either case you probably want to have several before you start cooking so you can replace them as necessary.

TIP If you have a good exhaust fan in your kitchen you can get smoky taste even without a barbecue grill. Take an iron or stainless roasting pan and cover the bottom with two layers of aluminum foil. Sprinkle fine bits of smoking wood over the whole surface, then cover that with more foil, leaving the edges open to the air. This goes on the lower shelf in the stove with your food on top. Tent both your main component and the smoking pan so that you keep as much smoke as possible inside. Turn up the oven to 350° F and turn on your exhaust fan.

There are ways to smoke without a smoker, but you always need a well-ventilated area for safety.

Smoking With Herbs and Spices

If you have an herb garden or access to fresh herbs and spices, they offer another way of bringing smoke to food, particularly items like fish that cook quickly. Just grab what you want—like fresh oregano, thyme, and basil—and toss them on the grill after you've started the main dish. Herbs cook quickly, so if you want them to extend the life span, go ahead and soak them in water.

You can also combine herbs and spices with smoking wood for a truly unique flavor profile.

Taking Up Smoking

Now you're ready to start. Determine what type of wood and size you want ahead of time so you have it on hand along with charcoal. By the way, it's perfectly acceptable to mix woods. I like using apple with oak, for example, as a way of toning down mesquite.

Create a layer of charcoal and heat it up. (You can use wood as your sole source of heat, but it's harder to manage temperatures with all-wood fires.) Whenever practical, use paper or sawdust and matches to start your fire. Accelerants are easy but they also have a residual smell and taste. An electric starter is a great option!

Charcoal Safety

On average you need about 30 pieces of charcoal to one pound of meat. Stack the charcoal in a pyramid shape. This provides enough ventilation for even burning. If you use lighter fluid, follow the directions on the can. Generally you need about ½ cup of fluid, letting the coal soak for a few minutes before lighting. The coals will be hot enough for smoking in about 30 minutes (they will have a white covering). Spread them out with edges overlapping/touching, and sprinkle your wood on top.

 Whenever possible use a natural fire starter to avoid lingering aromas and tastes left by accelerants.

Soak to Smoke?

There is a heated debate among grillers as to whether you have to soak your wood before using it for smoking. I am on both sides of the fence with this. I like soaking wood with beer, wine, and herbs that create another aromatic element along with unique flavor. However, scientifically speaking wood absorbs very little moisture over the span of a full day, let alone a few hours. Additionally when you put damp wood on your coals it changes the unit's internal temperature. What you see when you put damp wood on the fire is actually steam. The wood has to reach 575o F in order to begin producing smoke, so the wet wood increases the amount of time it takes to get your fire up and ready for smoking, which may leave you restocking charcoal along with your chosen wood.

Special Feature...

Walk the Plank!

The one exception to wood smoking is when you use wood planks. This type of cooking uses thin pieces of wood on which your main dish sets during cooking. The wood imparts flavor, but it needs to soak so it releases steam into your dish (and doesn't catch on fire!)

It is not necessary to soak wood before using it in your smoker. Doing so slows down the amount of time it takes to get the wood at a good rolling smoke.

Direct or Indirect

Generally speaking you want to set up your smoker for indirect heat. With direct cooking you put the food right over the heat source. With indirect cooking you design the heat source around the edges of your grill. This allows you to smoke the food slowly with the top of the grill closed (without fear of burning your food). If you're using a gas grill, turn on the side burners instead of the central and keep them low.

Too much Smoke?

Smoke reaches into your food down to about 1/8", just like a marinade. You have to be patient to get that much absorption. The thinner the cut, the more quickly it cooks, which is why whole bird (for example) has a ton of smoky flavor—it took longer to come to full doneness. There is no point at which your meat stops absorbing smoke. The key is basting lightly when you add more smoking wood. This helps hold the smoke on the surface and starts creating bark along with your rub. Remember—keep it light. You don't want to wash off the previous smoke layer, but rather give your meat enough moisture to hold the next round tight.

TIP As a beginner, I recommend that you pick out one kind of wood and use it exclusively for a while. You want to give your attention to your spices and temperature more than the wood, at least at first. If you don't pay attention to those elements, no amount of smoke will help your recipe.

Low and Slow

We have talked about this mantra previously in *Grilling for Beginners* and it's really important in smoking. You want to keep the wood smoldering. If you open your grill too frequently the wood tends to catch on fire from being exposed to fresh oxygen. Always remember to add wood at the outset of your cooking process when the meat is cold. Cold meat accepts smoke more readily. Additionally, the meal has the most time possible to absorb that aroma and flavor.

TIP A friend of mine brews beer using hand-smoked barley and grains that roast over cherry chips. You can also smoke tomatoes and use the resulting flavor to make unique sauces or salsa.

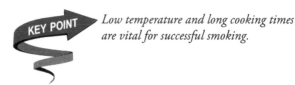

Low temperature and long cooking times are vital for successful smoking.

THE TAKEAWAY

- ▶ Brines and mops are good methods for keeping meat moist during the smoking process.

- ▶ Always use food-grade wood for smoking food. Do not use any wood of which you do not know the source.

- ▶ Use strong, heady woods on similarly strong flavored foods.

- ▶ Endeavor to use an electric or natural source for starting your wood on fire.

- ▶ It is not necessary to soak your smoking wood.

- ▶ Keep it low and slow, opening the unit as little as possible throughout the cooking process.

"Whether you are new to the scene or a long-time grillmaster, everyone has unique preferences when it comes to their cooking method of choice. From propane to charcoal to wood, people take their method of grilling quite seriously, and some argue quite passionately about the pros and cons of each method."

—Homaro Cantu, chef & molecular gastronomer

7

Fresh from the Rotisserie

A rotisserie is not an absolute necessity for beginning grillers, but it certainly is a fun toy that gives you another option for your menus. The beauty of the rotisserie is that it cooks your food evenly on all sides, not just the top and bottom like a conventional barbecue unit. The paced turning of the rotisserie provides you with a juicer end product because the motion helps your food self-baste.

continued...

Some grilling units come with a space for a rotisserie. They may even come with the add-on as part of the package. However, some rotisseries are self-sustaining (meaning you don't need a grill but can still get great barbecue flavor). Additionally you don't need as much meat for rotisserie cooking, making it a frugal option.

Special Feature...

Up, Down, Left, Right

Rotisseries come in two basic styles—vertical and horizontal. In a vertical rotisserie the meat heats from the side allowing a cook to remove slices as they finish as you might see in a gyro. The horizontal rotisserie is more common on the home front. It mounts on a table with a broiler or on a barbecue unit. The horizontal rotisserie requires balance—if the meat is mounted incorrectly it can interrupt the turn-drive or cause a jam.

KEY POINT

Rotisserie offers home chefs a cost-effective way of getting barbecue flavor and moist meat, often without a grill!

A Spin on History

No one knows for sure when the first person set up some sturdy branches, skewered some meat, and turned it slowly over the fire. What we do know is that they were readily used in fireplace designs. This set up was ideal for larger pieces of meat so that the meal slow-cooked in its own juices. Medieval kitchens in particular liked cooking this way—it was perfect for large gatherings and making a splashy presentation on the monarch's table. The person in charge of turning the meat was called a Spit Jack. Over time, however, clever inventers found other ways of powering the rotisserie (a word, that by the way, didn't appear until the Mid-1400s in France). The majority of modern units have mechanical motors for greater accuracy.

There is some disagreement between France and Italy as to who actually created little wind-up rotisseries for wood burning stoves, so I guess we can just give the credit to "Europe." Slowly, the mechanism spread to the United States, seeing a fair amount of household use. However, It seemed for a while American chefs overlooked the rotisserie. From about 1950 forward other barbecue methods caught their eyes like the Hibachi or a full gas grill. Nonetheless, it's making a comeback in a variety of sizes and styles, one of which is sure to fit your space and lifestyle.

Author's Aside

I fell in love with vertical rotisseries some years ago when I found a countertop version that had a special cooking unit on top for your side dishes. The vegetables cooked from the heat inside the unit while your meat turned at a pre-set pace of your choosing. My kids, to this day, call it the dancing chicken machine.

KEY POINT *The origins of rotisseries run consecutively and as elusively as barbecue grills. The modern rotisserie, however, is very easy to use and a great addition to your grilling tool kit.*

Special Feature...

Size Does Matter—Mammoth Rotisseries

Since 1881 one of the most popular attractions at Oktoberfest in Munich, Germany is a giant rotisserie, thanks to the efforts of a butcher by the name of Johann Rossler. This behemoth holds an entire ox.

The Guinness world book of records tells us the world's largest rotating grill, located in St. Wendel-Werchweiler, Germany, is 107' 8" long.

Selecting a Rotisserie

As previously mentioned, rotisseries come in sizes ranging from a small countertop model to huge commercial units like those used in certain restaurants and supermarkets. Obviously you need to consider your space constraints and whether your barbecue grill is set up for a rotisserie. There are some rotisserie brands that "retro" fit onto a unit even without the grill being constructed with that in mind. Always read your owner's manual to see what is possible and safe for the surface space you've got.

For those with outdoor pits, it's pretty easy to get free-standing manual or electric rotisseries. There is something primal about turning your own rotisserie but you won't get the same evenness as you would with an electric motor. When choosing an electric unit, look for one that's variable speed. You want to be able to cook large cuts like whole pigs very slowly (around 2 rpms). Faster speeds of around 6 rpm are kind of like the "standard operating temperature" in an oven (350 degrees F).

The advantage of variable speed is that it also gives you greater control over your food's exterior. You can start out on a higher speed to create a crust, then slow down the system, neatly keeping all those wonderful juices inside. No matter what, make sure you buy a suitably sized rotisserie for whatever type of food you're planning, including vegetables!

Rotisserie Grillied Vegetables

Special Feature...

There is a wonderful, inexpensive "add on" for your rotisserie and that's a grilling basket. There are two designs, a flat basket suitable for fish, and a tumble basket that has an easy-access door for your vegetables and other small items. Both attach in such a way that they rotate around the heat source in much the same manner as your main dish. Both types of baskets benefit from indirect heat so you reduce the chance of flair-ups or burning. Hint: you can lightly baste the vegetables as they cook to avoid drying too.

Besides a basket, another nice feature in a rotisserie is the addition of a drip pan. By the time you're done cooking all the juices are ready for your gravy or for use as a finishing sauce. As with your barbecue you'll still need some other accessories like a flavor injector, oven mitts, and baster.

Author's Aside

I know some enterprising folk who make their own rotisserie assemblies. Some are as simple as two big Y-shaped branches inserted firmly into soil on both sides of a cooking pit and a stainless steel bar with a grip for turning. Others get far more complex and creative. I, on the other hand, am mechanically challenged, so I stick to a commercial unit.

Buying Tips

The main piece of advice I give to new grillers is that since many rotisseries are indoor units you have to think about the landscape available. As long as you have suitable storage space for in between uses, then you're golden.

TIP If you have pets, I recommend making or buying a cloth appliance cover for the unit to keep it hair and dust-free between uses.

For practicality, look for a unit that's sturdy and easy to clean. Dishwasher safe parts are always a time-saving benefit. Also look for a system that has variable temperature controls and a timer if possible. Beyond that, here's your check list:

♦ ***Is the rotisserie large enough for the kind of food you cook?*** If you work with smaller cuts, you can get a smaller rotisserie. However, if you plan to entertain you'll find that size becomes a bit of an issue for feeding large groups.

♦ ***Convection or Radiant?*** Convection heat moves around the main dish. Radiant heat is stationary and the internal spit turns to expose different sides at an even pace.

♦ ***Spit: Look at the manner in which you have to load your food onto the spit.*** Is it clunky? Easy? Secure for the entire cooking process? You don't want your meat falling off, nor do you want to have to do yoga just to get it loaded properly.

♦ **Value added?** What type of accessories come in the package compared to other similarly sized rotisseries?

You have a lot of different options in rotisserie styles and features. Take your time and shop around until you find the one that best suits your space and cooking style.

Using Your Rotisserie

Meat doesn't tend to dry in a rotisserie compared to other types of cooking techniques. This means you can skip basting if you want to, but I confess that I'm a condiment snob—the more flavor, the merrier the meat. You can also use barbecue sauces and rubs on your creations, so a rotisserie is pretty flexible.

If you're planning on cooking whole birds, truss the legs and wings securely using butcher's twine. That keeps the tips from burning against the heat source. In this picture you can see a whole bird tied up neatly with bacon on the outside for even more flavor (I like to use cooked bacon for **poultry dressing**).

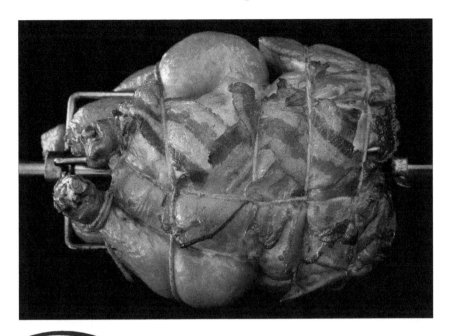

Shop Talk...

Dressing; N. A lot of people use the words "dressing" and "stuffing" interchangeably when, in fact, they are two different things. Dressing comes as a side dish prepared in a separate pan. Stuffing goes inside the bird and absorbs the flavors from injections, juices and marinades. I usually ignore the linguistics—I just call both delicious!

For average cuts of meat, one pound requires 15 minutes on the rotisserie. This changes a bit from recipe to recipe so definitely read the instructions and keep an eye on your food. This is another instance where an internal meat thermometer comes in handy.

Once you're done cooking and the rotisserie cools don't skimp on the cleanup. Just like your grill, this piece of equipment has little nooks and crannies where bits of food debris may hide, so give it a good wipe down, putting dishwasher-safe parts in the sanitation run.

Round and Round: What to Cook on the Rotisserie

There's a whole world of food that you can cook on your rotisserie depending on its size. It's truly ideal for larger cuts of meat. Think whole chicken, turkey and game birds, pork loin, or whole big, large roasts or shoulder cuts, game meat like venison, geese, and duck, and leg of lamb. That's just for starters!

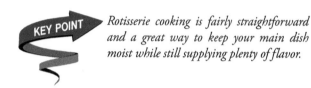

KEY POINT *Rotisserie cooking is fairly straightforward and a great way to keep your main dish moist while still supplying plenty of flavor.*

Tasty Rotisserie Tricks

Here are some simple tips and tricks that will make your rotisserie efforts more successful from the get-go.

1. Balance is everything. You need your meat securely on the skewer and fastened in place so there's no slipping or sliding. This also reduces wear and tear on your rotisserie motor.

2. Fire it up. Remember that you don't need as much heat with a rotisserie. With charcoal grills, put the hot coals around the edges of the unit leaving the area beneath the meat open. For gas grills either keep your burners on low, or only light the side burners away from the rotisserie.

3. If possible, set up the rotisserie so it spins away from you and use the open space in the middle of the charcoal grill for your drip pan (makes for easy access)! Add fresh charcoal about every half hour to keep the heat consistent.

4. It doesn't matter how great the cookbook or recipe, all cooking times are estmates. Every grill cooks a little differently (some hotter, some colder) and weather conditions also impact cooking times This is why it's good to have a meat thermometer. On the following page are some general cooking times for a <u>covered</u> grill rotisserie/safe internal temperatures for your reference.

Safe internal temperatures

Meat	Weight	Internal Temperature	Est. Time
Chicken	3 pounds	**165**	75 minutes
Lamb	5 pounds	**160 (well)**	2 hours
Beef Roast	3 pounds	**150 (medium)**	75 minutes
Pork Loin	3 pounds	**145**	1.5 hours

Stuffed turkey and other poultry require an extra 15 minutes of cooking per cup of stuffing added to reach a safe internal temperature.

WARNING!

5. Season your food before attaching it to the rotisserie. This is an excellent opportunity to try your hand with dry rubs.

6. Always stop the rotisserie about 15 minutes before the end of cooking time. The meat's temperature will continue to rise. This makes it easier to monitor the internal temperature of the food.

7. Let your meal rest for 10 minutes before carving it. This gives the internal juice time to even out throughout the cut.

8. The juice in your drip pan can be used as it stands or made into gravy by mixing it with a *roux*.

Shop Talk...

Roux; N. Roux is a mix of flower and some type of oil (butter, olive oil, chicken grease, etc.) The proportions are one Tbsp. melted butter to two Tbsp. of flour, mixed slowly together to form a paste. To this foundation you can add your pan drippings slowly for no-lump gravy. If you find you need more liquid, add stock or milk.

 Balance, seasoning, heat, and time are the four cornerstones of good rotisserie cooking.

THE TAKEAWAY

- ► Rotisseries create barbecue-like flavor at reasonable prices.

- ► Like a barbecue grill, the origin of the rotisserie is lost to history, but it remains an excellent addition to barbecue efforts.

- ► Shop around to find a rotisserie that's large enough for your family and entertaining needs and has all the features you want.

- ► Rotisserie cooking isn't hard and it keeps your main dish moist and flavorful.

- ► The keys to great rotisserie recipes are a balanced skewer, good seasoning blends, the right temperature and timing.

"The key to good grilling is to recognize that you are setting yourself up to cook in a whole new environment. This is actually one of the main purposes of grilling—to get yourself outside."

—Barton Seaver, world-renowned chef

8

History, Mystery and Myth

Home is Where the Heart(h) Is

Around the world, throughout the eras, people have assigned a special significance to the hearth (or heart) of the home. Our ancient ancestors gathered around community fires to share food, warmth, and safety. Fire was a potent friend or foe depending on the situation. *continued...*

Later, as civilization developed, humans transferred the beliefs surrounding communal fires to the kitchen (or pantry). These bits of folklore are among the most beloved in the world because they speak of tradition, culture, and family.

I want to share some of the history, myths and superstitions surrounding cooking fires. Some of these tidbits are great for sharing at any cookout.

 Keep a small notebook with a few of your favorite bits of barbecue and fire trivia. Take this with you to your next cookout to amaze and amuse like-minded grillers.

You may be wondering why you should read about our ancestors' feelings toward fire. Why explore their myths that tie to outdoor cooking?

Myths are meditations on the fundamental questions of human existence. How did we get fire in the first place? Who first thought of using it for cooking? When exploring any new pastime, the folklore and beliefs around it enrich your experience and broaden your understanding.

Fire & Food: Prehistory to Present

Anthropologists tell us that hearths started appearing around 300,000 years ago. The origin of fire, however, is far more elusive. If I may indulge in some light-hearted speculation, it's possible that a lightning bolt set a tree or other dry item on fire, probably scaring a poor cave person nearly to death. Even in that moment of fear, however, the warmth and light from the fire would have been quite a curiosity.

Upon repeated observation one or more of those ancient people figured out how to capture and control fire. Let's call this first adventurous soul Og. Can you imagine the greeting Og received upon returning to the cave with something so powerful...So useful? Fire became a defining moment. It is the foundations of clans, cultures and societies, and of course our food.

The discovery of fire revolutionized the way in which humans lived and interacted. Historians universally credit fire as the backbone of civilizations around the world. It provided warmth, light, safety, a means of manipulating the environment, and enabled humans to begin eating safer food by burning off harmful elements.

At first people probably gathered fire and held it in a safe place, feeding it with anything they could find that was dry. It would take some years before the idea of actually "creating" fire developed in part because our ancestors revered it. It would taken even longer before myths about fire developed, but there's no question that many reflect a sincere respect for the element of fire. The idea of "not playing with fire" isn't just your mom's good advice—it was about the spirit of the fire in which the ancients believed—it was truly sacred. In a tribal setting, a shaman typically became the caretaker of the flame because he or she alone could control that element safely.

Thankfully for us modern cooks, human inquisitiveness got the best of Og and his crew. Eventually experiments led to the use of fire in the hearth. Actually, our great hero Og may have been a heroine. In hunter-gatherer societies, men go out searching for meat while women tend the home, so the very first great grill master in history could very well have been female.

Author's Aside

*My husband's grandmother taught him to bake, so he shares our oven. The barbecue grill, on the other hand, is wholly mine. I let people use it begrudgingly, but I confess a sense of protectiveness over my personal fire festival. This is the venue from which I adore serving everything from innovative **fusion food** to doctored leftovers. If you've got more than one budding barbecue student in the house, you may want two grills!*

Shop Talk...

Fusion Food: Noun. Fusion cooking embodies the idea that food changes life and life changes food. It is the mixing and mingling of cultures, regions and individuals—typical Eastern cuisine meets West, North, South and everyplace in between. Wolfgang Puck is often credited with giving fusion flavors a public forum. One common example of fusion in the United States is Tex-Mex.

Obviously we have come a long way from rudimentary animistic beliefs toward the elements and just tossing meat into the flame and hoping for the best. The history of barbecue as we now know it is linked most closely to the Colonial period in the Western world. As people travelled, they made pits and functional cooking stands out of necessity. Unlike our modern customs, the grill was about functionality and survival, not entertaining. Even then, fire remained a constant companion to explorers, offering all the same value it gave their ancestors before them with a little more technological know-how.

Special Feature...

The Early Beginnings of Barbecue Equipment

Historians believe that spit cooking over wood came into common use shortly after the start of the Iron Age. Homer mentions long cooking forks used for treating meats at feasts in the Iliad and the Odyssey. Even the Bible alludes to barbecue-style equipment but at this juncture it was being used as a surface for burnt offerings.

The word "barbecue" first appeared in the Dictionary of the English Language by Samuel Johnson in 1755.

Fast forward to our lives today. You can easily see numerous types of grilling styles and **flavor profiles**. Be it Memphis or Kansas City, Buffalo or Oregon, everyone you meet knows someone who knows SOMETHING about barbecue (typically with bragging rights). No one "owns" grilling. It is a human tradition meant for communal enjoyment. That's the beauty and mystery of fire.

Shop Talk...

Flavor Profile: N or V. A flavor profile is like a fingerprint for your taste buds. When someone makes a recipe, they're designing it to have a distinct, dependable flavor. For example, fried rice typically has an Asian profile, but there is no reason it could not be transformed into an Italian dish by changing spices. This is considered "imparting" a flavor profile in a unique way.

So what about commercialization? In the United States, the outdoor grill first appeared in 1950, created by Don McLaughlin of the Chicago Combustion Corporation. It was called the Lazy Man, and had an open fire construction that integrated lava rock. The same company made a portable gas grill in 1954. It wasn't until 1966, however, that Philip Arnold founded Charmglow and began distributing grills for home use—and resurrected one of humanity's most ancient traditions in billions of backyards, decks, and patios all around the world.

Fire from Heaven

If you have ever read any Greek mythology you know about Prometheus stealing fire from the gods and giving it to humans. This particular mythic theme appears in a wide variety of other cultures around the world. The Native Americans tell us that humans had fire for a time until it was stolen away. A spirit animal (sometimes Coyote, sometimes Bear) becomes the hero in the story and gathers more embers from a mountain of fire and delivers them back to the tribe. Africans and Brazilians have similar tales, each featuring either a trickster or animal that helps humans claim their treasure.

Of course, fire isn't the only element about barbecue that appears in folk stories. Cooking and specific foods also play an integral role in teaching specific lessons in fables. Perhaps the most famous of these that has minor variations in the telling depending on the country, is Stone Soup.

The classic version tells of travelers who happened upon a very poor village, but did not wish to share their food because of the long road ahead. In response to this, several villagers set up a fire pit, filled a cauldron with water, and began bringing stones one at a time to the pot. They explained that they were making stone soup, but it needed a bit of savory assistance. Eventually each traveler contributed to the mix, and everyone enjoyed a hardy meal. In this case "too many cooks" were a good thing!

Author's Aside

When I read this story I cannot help but think of modern potluck dinners. If you want to have a theme barbecue, call it Stone Soup for the Grill and have everyone contribute something for the meal. Let each person use your grill and share their personal favorite technique or taste with everyone.

I am sure you can think of many other stories where fire and food play important roles, often emphasizing the significance of sharing and community. Barbecue can be like that too. That's why many parks and campgrounds offer communal barbecue pits. It creates the perfect environment to meet new people and enjoy good food.

The beauty here is that such stories can, indeed, become your own real life re-counting of a special experience at the grill—friends announcing a baby or marriage, your surprise anniversary barbecue, etc. There are so many special moments, and the barbecue is a perfect place to gather together and celebrate.

Blazing Beliefs: Superstitions About Fire, Hearth & Barbecue

Superstition abounds in every area of life, from marriage traditions and growing crops to numbers and pets. So it's not surprising to find a plethora of beliefs about fire, the hearth and even barbecue competitions.

Superstitious beliefs usually have both positive and negative sides. On the negative, dreams of fire are usually considered bad portents of sickness, fights, or family trouble. On a more positive note, Southern dream lore tells us that dreaming of a big fire occurs before some type of financial boost.

The Japanese have an interesting belief: they tell children that playing with fire makes them wet their beds. Now that's creative parenting!

Special Feature...

Fire Divination

In Europe, the ashes from a fire were sometimes used for a type of divination called ceneromancy. The interpretive value of patterns and mounds varied by culture. This was different from spodomancy, which reviewed the remains from sacred fires, and tephramancy that utilized the remnants of specific trees.

In times past, those who built houses often searched for just the right place for a hearth fire. It should never be in direct sunlight if you want it to light properly. It should also not stand on any ground with a history of misfortune. However, should the builder find a coin, or crystal, or four-leaf clover that indicated the favor of the local land spirits, that was a good sign that the home would be a happy, safe place.

Once built, the hearth continued in importance. In fact, our modern custom of housewarming gifts started long ago. When a young man moved away from home in ancient Greece, a bit of the hearth fire went with him. This was a way of taking his ancestry and love with him into a new life.

Author's Aside

In our neck of the woods (New England), this custom goes beyond just housewarming. It's considered proper to take a small gift for a host or hostess the first time you are invited to their house.

There are numerous superstitions about specific types of food and eating utensils that could be extended to the grill. For example, if you drop your cooking fork it means you'll have a female visitor soon, whereas dropping your cooking knife portends male company. When grilling hot peppers make sure to let your guest pick their own portion. Serving it to them directly causes discord.

The folklore and superstitions surrounding fire reflect early humankind's reverence toward this element, and provide cultural peeks into how early people explained fire's creation.

On New Year's, consider cooking up some honey-coated apple slices on a low flame for a sweet future. European custom says cooking and storing your bread upright is best for good fortune. Keeping garlic in your pocket, near the hearth or grill protects you from the Evil Eye. If you happen to cook barefoot, remember to put your shoes face up. Turning them downward invokes malicious energy. I could prattle on but I think you get the idea.

So what about barbecue? Well, despite our highly technological society, many grillers (particularly those who compete) have their own unique superstitions. Some have to use a specific rub or musical background. Others wear "lucky shirts" or use a specific knife that's only for the final presentation. If you trundle around in various barbecue chat rooms you'll find side conversations about these habits. Do they work? Who knows? But superstition is a way of instilling greater confidence, which usually has a positive outcome, even if it's not a blue ribbon.

THE TAKEAWAY

▶ The discovery and control of fire revolutionized human civilization and advanced human development in significant ways.

▶ The folklore and superstitions surrounding fire reflect early humankind's reverence toward this element, and provide cultural peeks into how early people explained fire's creation.

"Grilling, broiling or barbecuing—whatever you call it, it's an art. It's not just a matter of building a pyre and throwing on a piece of meat as a sacrifice to the gods of stomach."

—James Beard

9

Recipes

What would *Grilling for Beginners* **be without** a handy set of recipes to get you started on the right foot? I will be honest here in that I decided on this selection based on what I most enjoy cooking outdoors, however there are numerous resources for a greater variety of recipes offered in the "Deep Dish" portion of this book. You can also let your fingers do the walking over your handy keyboard and do some internet searches that focus on specific ingredients you'd like to use.

Sauces

Half the pleasure from good barbecue is getting to lick the sauce off your fingers as you go. While you can certainly run to your local market and pick up a bottle of your favorite commercial sauce, there's a lot to be said for making your own. When you want flavors that satisfy your cravings, homemade is the way to go. In all fairness, there are some truly delicious commercial products that offer not only flavor but time-savings. There is nothing wrong with reaching for that jar if you don't want to make your own. However, you also have the alternative of doctoring that commercial sauce to make it more personal.

So what makes for a great barbecue homemade or commercial sauce? One that has balanced flavor, that sticks to your key ingredient, and that adds to the experience versus covering up the star of the show completely. Nearly every sauce recipe contains acid, sugar, and spices. Contrary to what you might think, however, not all barbecue sauce has to be red. You can even find green sauce (often made with tomatillos as a base), a yellow sauce based in mustard, a brown sauce with soy and many other variations.

Author's Aside

As you develop sauces that everyone enjoys, consider making them in large batches for canning and freezing. Cook once, eat many times and have jars of scrumptious sauce left over for any meal or gift giving.

Basic Barbecue Sauce

This sauce is what most people think of when they think barbecue sauce. It is ketch-up-based with vinegar and some type of sweet element. We add spices and a little liquid smoke to lend smokiness without special equipment. Note that this blend, like most grilling sauces, can be used on the side for dipping, and makes great sandwich sauce!

Time: 15-20 minutes
Difficulty: ★★☆☆☆
Yields: 6 cups
Shelf Life: 2 weeks

Equipment

♦ Mixing Bowl
♦ Whisk or Spoon
♦ Nonstick Cooking Pan
♦ Storage Container

Ingredients

• 4 c ketchup
• ⅔ c brown sugar
• ⅔ c vinegar (your choice)
• ½ c black strap molasses
• 2 tbsp. Worcestershire sauce
• 2 tbsp. stone ground mustard
• 3 cloves garlic, minced
• 3 tsp. smoked paprika
• ½ tsp. black pepper
• ¼ tsp. celery salt
• ¼ tsp. onion powder
• ½ tsp. liquid smoke (optional)

Directions

1. Thoroughly mix all ingredients in bowl.
2. Transfer mixture to non-stick cooking pan.
3. Cook over low heat for 15 mins until ingredients are well integrated. Serve warm or cold.

TIP Different vinegars alter the flavor of your basic sauce. Cider vinegar has a fruity-tart appeal, wine vinegars are mellow and full-bodied, aged balsamic has a woody sweet taste, Rice vinegar is mild and smoky, and malt vinegar (as the name implies) tastes malty. Other vinegars you may find in specialty stores include coconut, raspberry, and beer just to name a few.

Basic barbecue sauce consists of a sugar, an acid and a foundation like ketchup to which cooks add a variety of spices based on personal taste and experience. The best barbecue sauces are those that stick to the main component and don't overwhelm any other flavors in your meal.

Special Feature...

Benefits of Barbecue Sauce

Sure it tastes great but did you know that many of the components in barbecue sauce are good for you too? A ketchup-based sauce has Vitamins A, C, and E along with minerals and antioxidants that support a healthy immune system.

■ Substitutions

Everyone eventually runs out of a key ingredient at the exact wrong time. You go to the refrigerator and the kids ate the last of the ketchup, for example. You're down to the wire for dinner and don't have time to run to the store. What's the solution? See what else might work. In this case you could use a Catalina salad dressing and reduce the sugar levels in the sauce. Or, if you have canned tomatoes, run them through a food processor or blender for smoothness and use those instead.

■ Sweet or Savory?

Some like it hot—some not. We have a mixed bag of taste buds in our family so I generally keep a little of each type of sauce on hand. As you may have already guessed, you can also blend the two ideas together for something a little different. For the beginner, however, let's stick to something straight forward.

Vinegar Barbecue Sauce

Savory vinegar barbecue sauces are extremely popular in Texas and Carolina where people use the blend not only as a sauce but as a marinade and a **finishing sauce**. Vinegar is a carrier, so to speak—it helps get flavor into the meat. The only caution is making sure you have other flavors balancing out the potent essence of the vinegar (unless you're a die-hard vinegar fan).

Shop Talk...

Finishing Sauce; N: Finishing sauces get added to a recipe either in the last 10 minutes of cooking, or the cook might serve them alongside of the meal as a dipping sauce for an extra layer of flavor. Examples include a pepper sauce for chicken, a wine sauce for grilled vegetables, and a pear sauce for gilled fruit or pork.

The typical vinegar sauce does not contain tomato (in fact, that's nigh unto a sin in some regions). It also varies from traditional barbecue sauce in that it's thinner. You'll see a lot of cider vinegar in old-time recipes but you can really use any vinegar you enjoy so long as it pairs well with your spices.

Vinegar Sauce

This sauce is perfect for poultry and vegetables. If time allows, make this (or any sauce) 24 hours in advance—as it sits in the refrigerator, the tastes mingle together for a happy marriage. Using spice powders produces results faster than coarse ingredients; if using coarse ingredients, give your sauce more steeping time.

Time: 15-20 minutes
Difficulty: ★★☆☆☆
Yields: 6 cups
Shelf Life: 2-3 weeks

Equipment
♦ Mixing Bowl
♦ Whisk or Spoon
♦ Nonstick Cooking Pan
♦ Storage Container

Ingredients
• 2 ½ c vinegar (your choice)
• 2 c filtered water
• 2 tbsp. white sugar or honey
• 2 tsp. each salt and pepper
• 1 stick butter
• 2 tsp. lemon juice
• 2 tbsp. Worcestershire sauce (optional)

Directions
1. Thoroughly mix all ingredients in bowl.
2. Transfer mixture to non-stick cooking pan.
3. Cook over low heat for 15 mins until ingredients are well integrated and butter is completely melted. Serve warm.

Sweet Barbecue Sauce

Sweet barbecue sauces often contain little, if any, hot spices. Rather they satisfy the sweet tooth using sugar, honey, **agave**, and/or fruit juices to achieve their flavor. While you can use artificial sweeteners in this kind of sauce if you wish, I don't recommend it—it's just not the same. Also, just because this is called "sweet sauce," you can still adjust your sweetening component to your personal tastes.

Shop Talk...

Agave; N: Known by the alternative name of Century Plant, Agave grows in Mexico where it is a chief component for tequila. Agave nectar comes from the flower stalk and acts as a sugar substitute.

Sweet Sauce

Sweet barbecue sauce can contain a tomato component if you wish. Here's one recipe for you to try (if you want a red sauce add about 3 Tbsp. ketchup; if you prefer it less sweet you can offset with white vinegar.) If you like, you can cook the sauce over low heat for 20 minutes to improve its depth.

Time: 10 minutes
Difficulty: ★★☆☆☆
Yields: 3 cups
Shelf Life: 2-3 weeks

Equipment
♦ Mixing Bowl
♦ Whisk or Spoon
♦ Storage Container

Directions
1. Thoroughly mix all ingredients in bowl.
2. Refrigerate until ready for use.

Ingredients
• ⅓ c honey
• ⅔ c molasses
• 1 c brown sugar
• ⅛ tsp. each ginger & cinnamon
• ½ tsp. smoked paprika
• 1 tsp. sea salt
• ¼ tsp. fresh ground pepper
• 1 clove garlic, minced
• ¼ c **brown sauce**
• 2 tbsp. Worcestershire sauce
• ½ tbsp. stone ground mustard
• ¼ cup fruit juice

Shop Talk...

Brown sauce; N: Brown sauce is a popular condiment in Britain that combines the flavors of Worcestershire and ketchup along with molasses, tomato, anchovies, and other spices depending on the brand. It's very similar to steak sauce and can be found in the same aisle at your supermarket.

Author's Aside

From personal experience I can tell you that sweet sauces can go from sumptuous to burnt very quickly. The sugar can cause flare-ups. Avoid this by cooking your food at a slightly lower temperature and by mindfully monitoring the dish from start to finish.

 KEY POINT *Both sweet and savory sauces serve a purpose in great barbecue. They give you ways of changing up your flavors while using a base that's still familiar and accommodating. Don't be afraid to mix the two from time to time and see what "secret" recipe you create!*

Glorious Global Sauces

If you've wandered the condiment aisle of your supermarket lately you've probably already noticed that barbecue sauce has come a long way from the basic blend. We now see influences from all over the world, particularly at international stores. The Internet also gives you access to a huge variety of recipe options from which to choose. So where do you want to virtually go today for a taste of something new? Spain? India? Mexico? Russia? The world is waiting at your doorstep!

The beauty of global cuisine is that you don't have to be a gourmet chef to get great results. In this section we'll look at two examples of Barbecue Sauce in different cultures—the Middle East and Eastern Asia.

■ A Taste of the Middle East

Middle Eastern cooking has a mix of herbs and spices that don't only create flavor but also color (you eat with your eyes!).

Some of the most common spices include:
- ◆ Cardamom
- ◆ Nutmeg
- ◆ Anise
- ◆ Allspice
- ◆ Garlic

- ◆ Cumin
- ◆ Turmeric
- ◆ Caraway
- ◆ Cinnamon
- ◆ Lemon

Middle Eastern Grilling

The word for "grill" in Arabic is Mangal, which literally translates as on the fire. This is because a lot of cooking takes place outdoors over coals. One example is shish taoouq, which skewers chunks of beef, lamb or chicken marinated with garlic, cumin, coriander, and lemon and grills them up. The meat may or may not receive sauce, but it certainly won't hurt the flavors. Sides for the dish include some type of garlic sauce, hummus, tabouli (a cracked wheat salad), and warm pita.

Mangal Sauce

This sauce is perfect with eggplant, mushrooms, and quail, but it's also great with steak and ribs. Don't worry about using your homemade basic barbecue sauce as a base for this recipe—a cheap, neutral store-bought brand will provide a great background for the traditional Middle Eastern flavors.

Time: 20 minutes
Difficulty: ★★☆☆☆
Yields: 1.5 cups
Shelf Life: 2-3 weeks

Equipment
♦ Mixing Bowl
♦ Whisk or Spoon
♦ Nonstick Cooking Pan
♦ Storage Container

Ingredients
• ⅓ c basic barbecue sauce
• ⅓ c pomegranate molasses
• 1 tsp. each butter and olive oil
• 1 tsp. flaked onion
• 2 tsp. minced garlic
• ½ lemon, fresh-squeezed for juice
• 1 tbsp. olive oil (separate)
• 1 tsp. each allspice and cinnamon
• ½ c beef or chicken stock
  (match to your meat)

Directions
1. Thoroughly mix all ingredients in bowl.
2. Transfer mixture to non-stick cooking pan.
3. Cook over low heat for 15 mins until ingredients are well integrated. Transfer to airtight container and cool until ready for use. Serve warm.

■ **East Meets West**

Chinese and Japanese culinary techniques and flavors have hit the "foodie" market in a significant way. From sushi stands with fried rice to Japanese Yakitori (barbecued skewered chicken thighs with leek), people everywhere seem to enjoy the heady flavors of Asian cooking.

Some traditional Asian sauce components include:

♦ Orange	♦ Ginger	♦ Sesame
♦ Soy	♦ **Hoisin**	♦ Star anise
♦ Rice vinegar	♦ Oyster sauce	♦ Fennel
♦ Five-spice powder	♦ Cinnamon	♦ Clove
♦ Cloves	♦ Garlic	♦ Hot pepper
♦ **Wasabi**	♦ **Yuzu citron**	♦ Mustard

Shop Talk...

Hoisin Sauce; N: A brown, somewhat sweet-spicy sauce with a consistency similar to ketchup. It's known by the alternative name "Peking" sauce. Primary ingredients for Hoisin include hot pepper, five spice powder, soybean, and sugar.

Wasabi; N: Wasabi is the Japanese equivalent of English horseradish. Common for use in sushi, sashimi, and soba, it's very aromatic and packs a wallop of flavor.

Yuzu Citron; N. Very similar to lime or lemon visually, Yuzu appears in baking and cooking equally. It's slightly tart, with orange and grapefruit hints and finds its way into many Asian dishes including syrup, vinegar, relish, sauces, and jelly.

Soy-Sesame Sauce

This is my favorite barbecue sauce with an Asian flavor profile. It goes well with flank steak, chicken, and pork. To boost the citrus flavor, consider adding Yuzo, orange zest, or even a little orange juice. Hint: Try this on cold Asian noodle salad or salad greens.

Time: 20 minutes
Difficulty: ★★☆☆☆
Yields: 1 cup
Shelf Life: 2-3 weeks

Equipment

♦ Whisk or Spoon
♦ Nonstick Cooking Pan
♦ Storage Container

Ingredients

- 1/3 c Hoisin sauce
- 4 tbsp. garlic rice vinegar
- 2 tbsp. soy sauce
- 1 tbsp. orange blossom honey
- 1/3 c shallot, finely minced
- 1 tbsp. each minced garlic and minced ginger (fresh)
- 2 tbsp. sesame seeds
- 1 tbsp. sesame oil
- 1/3 c sugar
- Pinch of five-spice powder
- 1/2 c beef or chicken stock (match to your meat)

Directions

1. Mix all ingredients in a non-reactive, non-stick cooking pan.
2. Cook over low heat for 15 minutes until sugar and honey completely integrate with other ingredients.
3. Taste test for sweetness; add sugar if desired.

KEY POINT

As you explore barbecue sauces from around the world you'll also have an opportunity to expose your taste buds to all kinds of herbs and spices, some of which you may have never even heard of. As you do, remember that food is a deep reflection of a people's culture, beliefs, and traditions.

The Color Wheel

At the outset of this chapter I mentioned that red is no longer the sole color to claim the attention of barbecue fans everywhere. There is literally a rainbow of flavors from which to choose. Here are just a few of my favorite recipes for your savory sampling pleasure.

KEY POINT *Creative use of color makes for pleasing barbecue presentations. In this case, you get both color and rich flavor.*

Carolina Yellow Barbecue Sauce

Carolina seems to be the queen of yellow barbecue sauces. This area was settled by German settlers who brought their love of good mustard with them. If you're interested in making your own **German mustard***, it's quite easy: All you need is mustard seed, vinegar, spices and a spice grinder.*

Time: 15 minutes
Difficulty: ★★☆☆☆
Yields: 4 cups
Shelf Life: 1 month

Equipment
♦ Mixing Bowl
♦ Whisk or Spoon
♦ Storage Container

Ingredients
- 3 c prepared German mustard
- 1 c malt vinegar
- ⅔ tsp. hot sauce
- 1 c white sugar
- 3 tsp. prepared chicken stock
- 2 tsp. celery seed
- 3 tsp. yellow mustard powder
- 2 tsp. dried rosemary leaves
- 2 tsp. minced dry onion
- 2 tsp. garlic powder
- 1 tsp. each savory salt and ground black pepper

Directions
1. Thoroughly mix all ingredients in bowl.
2. Chill for one hour. Serve cold.

Shop Talk...

German Mustard; N. There are several varieties of German-style mustard. One type uses roasted mustard seed with honey, apple juice, and vinegar for a sweet taste. Another starts with brown and yellow mustard seeds and horseradish for a spicy profile. The third uses mostly brown mustard seed for deeper flavor. Many German mustards are coarse ground.

Alabama White Barbecue Sauce

True to its name, this sauce is very popular in Alabama. While there are many variations (some thick like salad dressing and some thin like vinegar sauce), this is one recipe that seems to be a crowd pleaser. Because this recipe utilizes mayonnaise it's essential to keep it in the refrigerator until you're ready to apply it to the barbecue or serve it as a dipping sauce (otherwise it tends to separate). It's perfect with chicken.

Time: 15 minutes
Difficulty: ★★★☆☆
Yields: 3 cups
Shelf Life: 1 week

Equipment
♦ Mixing Bowl
♦ Whisk or Spoon
♦ Storage Container
♦ Food Processor or Blender

Ingredients
• 2 c mayonnaise
• 1 ½ c cider vinegar
• ¼ c corn syrup
• ⅛ tsp. chipotle pepper, ground
• 1 ½ tsp. horseradish
• 2 cloves garlic, finely minced
• 1 tsp. white sugar
• ⅛ c each white wine vinegar and water
• ½ tbsp. coarse ground black pepper
• ½ tsp mustard powder
• ½ tsp. liquid smoke

Directions
1. Add mayonnaise, white wine vinegar, spices and liquid smoke to blender or food processor. Mix thoroughly on medium speed.
2. Add remaining ingredients to blender and mix thoroughly until well-integrated.
3. Chill for one hour. Serve cold.

Orange Barbecue Sauce

As the name implies, this tasty sauce gets its color and flavor from oranges. The addition of chili powder or hot sauce provides a little heat to the orange's sweetness. It's great on chicken, pork, ribs and shrimp, but for something different, use this on grilled carrots or sweet potatoes.

Time: 15-20 minutes
Difficulty: ★★☆☆☆
Yields: 3 cups
Shelf Life: 2 weeks

Equipment
♦ Whisk or Spoon
♦ Nonstick Cooking Pan (saucepan)
♦ Storage Container

Ingredients
- 2 c orange marmalade
- 5 tbsp. fruit vinegar (not cider) or white wine vinegar
- 5 tbsp. Worcestershire sauce
- 3 tsp. chili powder or 2 tsp. hot sauce
- 1 c fresh squeezed orange juice
- 1 tbsp. light brown sugar
- 1 tbsp. honey

Directions
1. Mix all ingredients in large, nonstick sauce pan.
2. Simmer for 10 minutes.
3. Apply to barbecue in final 10 minutes of cooking and serve as dipping sauce.
4. Store leftovers in an airtight container in the refrigerator.

In the Pink Sauce

We make this sauce at home regularly for both a marinade and grilling sauce for chicken. This is perfect for grilled fruit, too. If you want to max out the berry flavor, swap out frozen strawberry margarita mix for the water.

Time: 15-20 minutes
Difficulty: ★★☆☆☆
Yields: 3 cups
Shelf Life: 2 weeks

Equipment
♦ Whisk or Spoon
♦ Nonstick Cooking Pan (*saucepan*)
♦ Storage Container
♦ Food Processor or Blender

Ingredients
• ½ cup white wine vinegar
• 1 tsp. aged balsamic vinegar
• 1 tbsp. Worcestershire sauce
• ½ tbsp. lemon or orange zest
• ½ c light brown sugar
• 1 tsp. white sugar
• 1 tsp. each onion and garlic, finely minced
• 1 tsp. white pepper
• ½ tsp. smoked paprika
• 2 c filtered water
• 2 c hulled strawberries

Directions
1. Mix all ingredients except for strawberries in a nonstick saucepan.
2. Simmer over low heat for 1 ½ hours, stirring regularly.
3. Meanwhile, prepare strawberries in food processor or blender—they should have some texture, but the chunks shouldn't be so large as to stick to your meat or grilled fruit.
4. Add berries to saucepan and simmer another ½ hour. Remove from heat and allow to cool for 15 minutes—the sauce will thicken in this time. Baste it onto your barbecue while hot.

Grilling Green Sauce

Green sauces are a staple of Tex-Mex cuisine. The blend is perfect for pork, chicken, and shrimp, and will really wake up your taste buds (they'll be doing a hat dance in no time!) Want to turn down the heat? Substitute Poblano peppers for the jalapenos.

Time: 1 hour
Difficulty: ★★☆☆☆
Yields: 4 cups
Shelf Life: 1 week

Equipment

♦ Baking Sheet
♦ Whisk or Spoon
♦ Nonstick Cooking Pan
   (*large saucepan*)
♦ Blender
♦ Storage Container

Ingredients

• 2 c green onion, chopped
• 1 c tomatillos, husked and minced
• 2 c tomatoes, cubed
• 1 medium onion, chopped
• 2 tsp. extra virgin olive oil
• 1 jalapeno pepper, seeded and sliced
• ¼ c cider vinegar
• ¼ c honey
• 2 tbsp. cilantro, minced
• 2 tbsp. tequila

Directions

1. Preheat oven to 400 degrees Fahrenheit.
2. Place tomatillos, onion, and jalapeno on a baking sheet. Sprinkle with olive oil and bake for 30 minutes, or until they begin caramelizing.
3. Combine remaining ingredients in saucepan. When baked ingredients are finished, add to saucepan and mix thoroughly.
4. Simmer for 1 hour, or until tomatoes and tomatillos are fork tender.
5. Cool to room temperature, then process in blender until sauce is smooth. Chill and serve cold.

Finishing Sauces & Dips

Realistically, all the recipes in this chapter could become a finishing sauce or dip for your barbecue. The real question is, how do you want to use them? Sometimes people prefer a lighter grill, meaning that they cook without sauce. In this case, using your sauces to finish the meal or just leaving it out for guests to add as they wish makes sense. The extra benefit of using your grilling sauces only for finishing sauce or dip is that you leave the main component to shine on its own.

Traditionally, a finishing sauce gets involved in the cooking process at the very end of the recipe's called-for cook time. Alternatively, you can drizzle it over the main ingredient after plating and just prior to service. You can use finishing sauce on anything you grill—it's really a matter of personal taste.

Here are some ideas for finishing sauces:

Beef
- ▶ Mushroom sauce
- ▶ Tomato, vinegar, brown sugar, and red wine
- ▶ Butter, apple juice, shallot, beef stock, garlic, and black pepper

Chicken
- ▶ Lemon pepper sauce
- ▶ Olive oil, white wine, garlic, orange zest, rosemary, and salt
- ▶ Chicken stock, onion, white wine, butter, and ginger

Fish
- ▶ White wine, shallots, parsley, butter, and lemon
- ▶ Fish stock, mushrooms, eggs, butter, heavy cream, and anchovies
- ▶ Mayonnaise, basil, onion, hot sauce, and dill relish

Pork
- ▶ Cider or malt vinegar, brown sugar, Cajun seasoning, black pepper, and parsley
- ▶ Olive oil, garlic, oregano, white wine, salt, and pepper
- ▶ Chicken stock, lime, white vinegar, shallots, kosher salt, and light brown sugar

Vegetables
- ▶ Fish sauce, lime juice, light brown sugar, cilantro, and fennel
- ▶ Hoisin sauce, orange juice, ginger, garlic, and sesame
- ▶ Olive oil, white wine, mustard, onion powder, and thyme

Fruit
- ▶ Apple juice, sparkling wine, and ginger **reduction sauce**
- ▶ Pomegranate, red wine, and chipotle
- ▶ Mango, white wine, pineapple juice, and sweet basil

Shop Talk...

Reduction Sauce; N. Making reduction sauces at home is very easy. It's simply a matter of simmering or boiling a sauce to reduce the amount of liquid. This, in turn, intensifies the flavor of your finishing sauce.

KEY POINT

Finishing sauces can be a traditional barbecue sauce applied at the end of cooking, or drizzled over top of a component prior to serving. They can also be wholly different creations that match your meal's flavor profile.

Special Feature...

Barbecue Myths

Like any other pastime, there are some common myths about barbecue that have turned into urban legends.

1. While searing caramelizes meat, it will not keep your meat from drying out if you overcook it. However, marinade helps keep meat moist even if it doesn't sink deep into your dish. And for those of you who avoid salting meat before you grill— quit worrying. It will not dry out the dish.

2. Just turning the heat on high will NOT clean your grill. You have to wash it thoroughly like any other kitchen implement to avoid foodborne illness.

3. Just because you're grilling doesn't mean you need sauce during cooking (thus the reason for finishing sauces and dips).

4. In terms of food safety you should NOT bring any meat to room temperature before cooking. It should stay in the refrigerator. Your grill will do a fine job of bringing up the meat's temperature all on its own.

Beef Recipes

Did you know that beef is good for you? The fat you see in beef is a type of oleic acid—the same yummy stuff that's in olive oil! That means that eating meat (within reason) actually supports overall health by decreasing bad cholesterol (LDL) and, in turn, supporting heart health. Beef has a variety of including iron and zinc, along with a hearty portion of Vitamin B. The other great advantage of grilling beef is that you can visibly see the amount of fat you'll eventually consume, so you can trim it if you want.

Luscious London Broil

This is a beautiful cut of meat that doesn't require a lot of dressing for a rich flavor.

Time: 30-40 minutes
Difficulty: ★★☆☆☆
Yields: Serves 3
Shelf Life: 3-4 days

Equipment

♦ Mixing Bowl
♦ Whisk or Spoon
♦ Food Storage Bag
♦ Grilling Tools

Ingredients

• 1 lb. London Broil (1½" cut)
• 4 cloves whole garlic
• 1 Tbsp. kosher salt
• ¼ cup cider vinegar
• ¼ cup sweet soy sauce
• 1 Tbsp. orange blossom honey
• 2 tsp. Worcestershire sauce
• 1 tsp. fresh ground black pepper

Directions

1. Put meat into food storage bag.
2. Mix all other ingredients in a bowl and add to storage bag.
3. Place in refrigerator for six hours, turning bag hourly.
4. Prepare grill for direct heat with a light coating of oil, then heat to 500 Fahrenheit.
5. Remove meat from marinade and drip off excess liquid. Set marinade aside.
6. Sear meat on the grill for five minutes on both sides.
7. Drop heat to 325 degrees and cook ten minutes on both sides.
8. When meat's internal temperature reaches 120 degrees, remove from heat and allow it to rest until the internal temperature reaches 130 degrees (medium rare).
9. Boil the marinade in a medium saucepan for basting or finishing.
10. Serve with crunchy potatoes or grilled vegetables.

Ribeye Steak

Ribeye is plain lovely. Sometimes called Scotch Fillet, this steak comes from the tastiest part of a cow, is naturally tender and typically boneless. When shopping for ribeye steaks, look for those that have plenty of fat marbling throughout the cut. This is also a good recipe for a gourmet salt—I recommend Himalayan.

Time: 15-20 minutes
Difficulty: ★☆☆☆☆
Yield: Serves 4
Shelf Life: 2-3 days

Equipment
♦ Mixing Bowl
♦ Whisk or Spoon
♦ Marinating Container
♦ Aluminum Foil
♦ Barbecue Tools

Ingredients
• 4 steaks (8 oz.)
• 2 c. Cabernet Sauvignon
• 1 tsp. liquid smoke
• 2 Tbsp. olive oil

Directions
1. Mix the wine and liquid smoke in bowl and pour into marinating container.
2. Soak each side of the ribeye for 10 minutes in the marinade.
3. Brush the grilling surface with olive oil and heat to high.
4. While grill warms, let steaks rest at room temperature.
5. Brush steaks with olive oil, and salt and pepper to taste.
6. Grill steaks for 4 minutes on each side.
7. Drop the temperature to medium heat and cook steaks for 5-7 minutes, or until internal temperature reaches 125-130 degrees (rare to medium rare).
8. Remove from heat and allow to rest under a tent of aluminum foil until internal temperature reaches 135-140 degrees (medium well).

KEY POINT

While a recipe may call for ground beef, you can substitute any other ground product you choose including game meats. Just remember to check internal temperature guidelines to insure that your food is cooked safely.

Barbecue Sliders

These little gems can be made with any type of ground meat, or even a mix of them. The recipe calls for buttermilk biscuits but if you can find small slider rolls at a local bakery, that would make an excellent substitution. Note that if your supermarket doesn't carry **apple slaw**, *a traditional coleslaw mix does just fine.*

Time: 25-30 minutes
Difficulty: ★★☆☆☆
Yield: Serves 5
Shelf Life: 2-3 days

Equipment
♦ Mixing Bowl
♦ Whisk or Spoon
♦ Aluminum Foil
♦ Barbecue Tools

Ingredients
- 1 ½ lbs. ground beef
- 1 egg
- ¾ c. seasoned bread crumbs
- 1 c. hickory barbecue sauce
- 1 c. Bourbon Hot Sauce
- 1 ½ c. apple slaw
- 10 buttermilk biscuits, cooked according to package directions

Directions
1. Thoroughly mix ground beef, egg and bread crumbs in a bowl.
2. Shape into five small patties (a little larger than your biscuits).
3. Mix barbecue and hot sauce together and set aside.
4. Brush the grilling surface with oil and heat to medium.
5. Sprinkle sliders with a little salt and pepper.
6. Grill sliders for 4 minutes on one side, then lightly brush with sauce blend.
7. Flip sliders and repeat the above step..
8. Remove from heat and cover for five minutes.
9. Serve on biscuits topped with sauce and apple slaw.

Shop Talk...

Apple Slaw; N. Thanks to the ever-growing culinary market, slaw is not just for cabbage any more. You can get broccoli and fennel versions. Apple slaw typically combines apple shreds, cabbage, and carrots with mayonnaise, vinegar, honey, and sometimes walnuts and cranberries for a great textural variety.

Chicken and Poultry

So now we know about beef benefits, but what about poultry? Generally, chicken and poultry are lower in fat than beef or pork. Besides this, chicken is high in zinc, calcium, niacin, and other trace minerals that support a healthy immune system. Children who have poor appetites benefit from eating grilled chicken as the amino acids in the meat helps growth. Additionally, chicken is a "comfort food"—the Vitamin B5 deters stress-related disorders.

Brined Chicken Legs

Chicken legs are really the only way I like dark meat in poultry. They're fun "finger foods" so you can grab a cooled leg and have it any time. Serve with Corona and a slice of lemon or other citrus fruit of your choosing

Time: 1 hour
Difficulty: ★★★☆☆
Yield: Serves 4
Shelf Life: 3-4 days

Equipment
♦ Mixing Bowl
♦ Whisk or Spoon
♦ Fork
♦ Food Storage Bag
  (or large covered container)
♦ Grilling Tools

Ingredients
• 2 Tbsp. salt
• ¼ cup Hawaiian sugar
• 1 Tbsp. minced garlic (fresh)
• 1 tsp. poultry seasoning
• 1 tsp. minced onion
• 1.5 quarts liquid*
• 4 Chicken legs
• 2 cups barbecue sauce (any)

* Water, beer, white wine or chicken broth will all work.

Directions

(PREP)
1. Mix the salt, sugar, garlic, poultry seasoning, onion and liquid together in a bowl. Make sure the salt is fully integrated.
2. Pierce the chicken with a fork on both sides.
3. Place the brine into a food storage bag or container with the chicken.
4. Leave in the refrigerator for at least two hours.

(COOK)
1. Prepare the grill with a coating of vegetable oil and heat it to 375° F.
2. Drain the chicken then move it to the grill.
3. Cook on each side for 7 minutes without sauce.
4. Coat each side of the legs and return them to the grill for another 20 minutes, turning regularly. Apply barbecue sauce on each turn.

Tipsy Cornish Game Hens

Game hen has a delicate flavor that's richer than chicken. Their size makes them the per-fect portion for one person (no guesswork on how many to buy). This also means less cooking time than a whole turkey or chicken. They make a great main dish.

Time: 1 hour
Difficulty: ★★☆☆☆
Yield: Serves 3
Shelf Life: 3-4 days

Equipment

♦ Mixing Bowl
♦ Whisk or Spoon
♦ Paper Towels
♦ 3 Empty Beer Cans
♦ Metal Shears
♦ Grilling Tools

Ingredients

• 1 garlic clove minced
• 1 tsp. onion powder
• 1 cup balsamic vinegar
• 1 cup smoky barbecue sauce
• 1 cup dark beer
• 3 Cornish Game Hens
• Vegetable oil
• Barbecue rub*
• Salt and pepper to taste

* Hickory or lemon pepper are nice, but you can use any commercial chicken rub.

Directions

(PREP)

1. Wash the hens inside and out, then pat with a paper towel.
2. Brush the hens with oil and then apply the barbecue rub.
   Let them sit in the refrigerator overnight.
3. Mix together the garlic, onion, vinegar and barbecue sauce.
4. Remove the top from the beer can.
5. Cut the beer cans in ½.
6. Preheat grill to medium-hot.
7. Fill the cans with the sauce mixture.
8. Place each hen on top of one can by inserting the can in the cavity.
9. Move the hens with the cans to the grill—distribute evenly over indirect heat.

(COOK)

1. Grill on medium-high for 10 minutes to crisp up the skin (watch this carefully as hen can burn depending on the size)
2. Reduce to medium heat and continue cooking for 1 hour or until the internal temperature reaches 165o.

Serving Suggestion: Use any leftover sauce for dipping. Consider making bacon flavored dressing as a side dish.

KEY POINT *Chicken is perhaps the most adaptable meat you'll ever "meet." It accepts flavors readily, making it an ideal background for outstanding barbecue sauces and rubs.*

Skewered Chicken Breasts

Kabobs are always a crowd pleaser. You can get your guests involved (if you wish) by picking out the ingredients for their skewer. Fix them up as a main dish and use the marinating time for visiting!

Time: 12-15 minutes
Difficulty: ★★☆☆☆
Yield: Serves 6
Shelf Life: 3-4 days

Equipment
♦ Mixing Bowl
♦ Whisk or Spoon
♦ Food Storage Bag
♦ Skewers
♦ Grilling Tools

Ingredients
• 4 boneless chicken breasts
• ⅓ cup honey
• ⅓ cup soy sauce
• ¼ cup rice vinegar
• ½ cup pineapple juice
• 1 Tbsp. minced garlic
• 2 large onions cut in 2" pieces
• 2 sweet peppers cut in 2" pieces
• 1 dozen medium brown mushrooms (washed)
• 1 dozen 2" cubes fresh pineapple
• Heirloom Cherry Tomatoes *

Purple, yellow and orange make a very visually appealing presentation

Directions

(PREP)
1. Mix the ingredients together and place them in an airtight food storage bag.
2. Place the bag in the refrigerator for 4 hours, turning every hour for even marinating.

(COOK)
1. Drain the chicken, reserving the liquid if you want to baste during grilling.
2. Boil the baste before using it on the grill.
3. Lightly oil the grill and turn it to medium.
4. While the grill warms, thread the meat and vegetables on to the skewers, alternating the order of ingredients (meat, onion, mushroom, tomato, pepper, pineapple—repeat…or whatever you like.)
5. Cook on the grill for about 15 minutes, turning the kabobs every five minutes. Add a bit of baste on every turn (if you're using it.)
6. The chicken juices should run clear when the kabobs are done.

This is really great with a wild rice pilaf, to which you add slivered almonds or cashews.

Pork

Pork offers a relatively low-calorie meat choice, particularly when compared to beef sirloin, which is nearly twice as caloric for a similar portion. Like other meat, you get a solid helping of protein (as much as one egg per ounce of pork.) It is an ideal choice for people on a low-cholesterol or low-carb diet because it's much lower than beef in its cholesterol levels—and like other meats, pork has no carbs.

KEY POINT *Pork is a carbohydrate-free meat—so get rid of the guilt and grab a napkin!*

Brined Pork Chops

This brine creates a light fruity flavor in your pork chops and also helps keep them moist. You can change the flavor of the juice as desired (pineapple-orange is always a winner). Note that you can increase the number of servings you'll get from this main dish recipe simply by doubling or tripling the basic ingredients.

Time: 30 minutes
Difficulty: ★★☆☆☆
Yield: Serves 2
Shelf Life: 3-4 days

Equipment
♦ Mixing Bowl
♦ Whisk or Spoon
♦ Food Storage Container
♦ Grilling Tools
♦ Oil
♦ Meat Thermometer

Ingredients
• 2-8oz center cut pork chops
• ½ quart mango or passion fruit juice
• ½ quart ice water
• ⅛ cup kosher salt
• ⅛ cup white or brown sugar
• Black pepper (coarse ground)

Directions

(PREP)
1. Mix the juice, water, salt and sugar together in a bowl or food storage container.
2. Add the chops to the brine so that they're completely covered.
3. Refrigerate the pork in the brine for at least one hour.

(COOK)
1. Prepare the grill by pouring out and arranging your coals in a pile on one side of the unit. Light them and wait until they turn evenly white. *continued...*

2. Put the cooking grate in place and oil it lightly.
3. Drain the pork chops, and pat them dry using paper towels.
4. Rub the black pepper into both sides of the meat, taking personal tastes into account.
5. Place the meat on the hot part of the grill for four minutes each side.
6. Move the meat to the cooler side of the grill. Insert a meat thermometer into the thickest portion of one chop. When the meat reaches 135o, remove it.
7. Let stand for 10 minutes before serving.

Serving Suggestion: My favorite side dish for this recipe is green bean casserole, and if you're looking to pair with a nice wine, I recommend a sweet Zinfandel as a counterpoint to the natural saltiness that the pork will absorb from the brine.

Baby Back Ribs!

Baby Back Ribs

I have spent years endeavoring to create perfect, fall-off-the-bone ribs. What I discovered is that a lot depends on both the quality of the meat as well as the overall process. This recipe combines baking with grilling for a slow-cooked tenderness.

Time: 1 hour 45 minutes
Difficulty: ★★★☆☆
Yield: Serves 4
Shelf Life: 3-4 days

Equipment

♦ Mixing Bowl
♦ Whisk or Spoon
♦ Roasting Pan with Rack
♦ Paper Towel
♦ Knife
♦ Aluminum Foil
♦ Grilling Tools

Ingredients

• 4 Pounds of baby back ribs
• 2 Tbsp. Hawaiian sugar
• 1 tsp. mustard powder
• 1 Tbsp. smoky paprika
• 1 tsp. each salt & pepper
• 1 tsp. chipotle powder
• 1 tsp. garlic powder
• 1 tsp. onion powder
• 1 tsp. Worcestershire powder (optional)
• Liquid
• 2-3 bay leaves

Directions

(PREP)

1. Preheat the oven to 350°.
2. Unwrap your ribs and turn them face down.
3. Using a knife point, loosen the membrane from the back of the ribs. Take a paper towel in hand and use it for gripping. Pull the membrane off and discard it.
4. Mix together all your dry ingredients except for the bay leaves.
5. Rub this mixture evenly over both sides of the ribs.

(COOK)

1. Fill the bottom of a roasting pan with a liquid of your choice (*water, wine, beer, juice etc.*). Make sure this does not go above the internal cooking rack.
2. Place the rib racks side by side on the cooking rack. Cover the pan with aluminum foil.
3. Turn down the oven to 300° and bake for 75 minutes, until the meat begins to retreat from the bone.
4. Transfer the ribs to a medium-heat grill.
5. Cook on both sides for 15 minutes.
6. If you want to use sauce, add it during the last five minutes or serve it as a finishing dip.

Serving Suggestion: A classic dish deserves classic sides:
Go with potato fries and grilled asparagus.

Barbecued Ham

A whole bird isn't the only larger cut of meat suited to the grill. A cured, spiral cut ham really benefits from indirect heating, particularly if combined with apple or apricot smoking wood. Serve as a main dish.

Time: 40 minutes
Difficulty: ★★★☆☆
Yield: Serves 4-5
Shelf Life: 3-4 days

Equipment

♦ Mixing Bowl
♦ Whisk or Spoon
♦ Spatula
♦ Grilling Tools
♦ Aluminum Foil
♦ Smoking Wood (*optional*)*
♦ Meat Thermometer

*Many hams are pre-smoked, but you can add wood to the charcoal to enhance that flavor

Ingredients

• 4 pound precooked spiral ham
• 1 cup apricot jam
• 1 cup chicken broth
• Butter (optional)

Directions

(PREP)

1. Remove the skin and fat from the ham, leaving only a little fat for cooking.
2. Prepare the glaze by mixing the apricot jam with the broth (you can add spices like clove or cinnamon to this if desired.)
3. Preheat the grill to 225° F on the indirect side.
4. Toss wood on the hot part of the grill.

(COOK)

1. Put the ham on the grill surface over the indirect heat, with the flat side down.
2. Smoke the meat for one hour.
3. Remove the meat temporarily, covering it with a layer of aluminum foil. Hint: you can add more broth (or a little butter) between the spiral cuts for moisture.
4. Return it to indirect heat until your meat thermometer reaches 130°.
5. Open the tin foil and layer the ham with the glaze.
6. Close your unit and let the glaze set for 10 minutes.
7. Baste the ham from the drippings gathered in the aluminum foil.
8. At this point, you can move the ham to the hotter part of the grill and tighten up the glaze even further. This process won't take long, but watch it closely as the sugars can burn.

9. Check the internal temperature again after about 4 minutes of
10. cooking the glaze. It needs to be 140°.
    Let the meat rest, then slice for serving. Retain the drippings as a
    finishing sauce.

Serving Suggestion: Roasted leeks and baby vegetables are great sides,
and rosé is a perfect pairing wine.

Fish

The Mayo Clinic advocates eating 2 helpings (7oz.) of fish weekly in order to benefit from the high levels of Omega 3 fatty acids that promote heart health and reduce the risk of heart disease. Fish is also a great source of protein. Some of the best fish for your health include wild salmon, Atlantic mackerel, rainbow trout and albacore tuna.

Firm fish is better for barbecuing. If you use a more delicate fish like tilapia it's best to use a non-stick fish grilling basket, which you can find at most department stores with the other barbecue equipment.

Plank-Grilled Salmon

Being a firm fish, salmon holds up really well on the grill. The light flavor of the oak comes through and mingles with the herbs in this main dish recipe, but there is no reason you can't experiment with other plank flavors, like apple, cherry, and hickory.

Time: 20-30 minutes
Difficulty: ★☆☆☆☆
Yield: Serves 4
Shelf Life: 2-3 days

Equipment

♦ Mixing Bowl
♦ Whisk or Spoon
♦ Cedar Planks*
♦ Grilling Tools

*You can use one large plank if it fits all four fillets.

Ingredients

• 1 -1/2 pounds skin-on salmon cut in four equal pieces*
• Extra Virgin olive oil
• 6 Tbsp. honey mustard
• Salt, pepper and Dill to taste
• Apple cider**

**You can cook the salmon whole, if you prefer; it will just take a little longer
**** Alternatively, a lemon-flavored wine (like that from Lemon Creek).

Directions

(PREP)

1. Soak the cedar plank in the cider or wine for two hours before your planned cooking time.
2. Rub the entire outside of the fish with a light coating of oil.

TIP Grilling planks are reusable until they crack or scorch badly. Wash them thoroughly after each use, and let them dry. If it's going to be a while before my next barbecue, I treat mine with olive oil so they retain their finish.

3. Mix the mustard, salt, pepper and dill. Rub this into the surface of the salmon and set aside while you prepare your grill.
4. Preheat your barbecue unit to medium heat (350°).

(COOK)
1. Fill the bottom of a roasting pan with a liquid of your choice (water, wine, beer, juice etc.). Make sure this does not go above the internal cooking rack.
2. Place the rib racks side by side on the cooking rack. Cover the pan with aluminum foil.
3. Turn down the oven to 300° and bake for 75 minutes, until the meat begins to retreat from the bone.

Sweet Tart Basil Halibut

When shopping for halibut, watch for filets that are translucent and have a clean scent. This firm fish, like salmon, holds together wonderfully on the grill. Be careful not to overcook this main dish—that dries it out. On average, you need 10 minutes per 1" thick steak, turning the fish only once.

Time: 10-15 minutes
Difficulty: ★★☆☆☆
Yield: Serves 3
Shelf Life: 3-4 days

Equipment
♦ Mixing Bowl
♦ Whisk or Spoon
♦ Sauce Pan
♦ Long-Handled Barbecue Brush
♦ Grilling Tools

continued...

Ingredients
• 3-6 ounce Halibut steaks
• 2 Tbsp. Olive oil
• 2 Tbsp. Butter
• 2 Tbsp. fresh crush garlic
• 2 Tbsp. Brown sugar
• ½ tsp. Lemon zest
• 2 tsp. dried basil
• 2 tsp. soy sauce

Directions

(PREP)

1. Mix oil, butter, garlic, sugar, lemon zest and basil together in a bowl.
2. Transfer to a sauce pan.
3. Warm over low heat until the ingredients are fully integrated.

(COOK)

1. Prepare the grill with a coating of oil on the grates, then heat to medium high.
2. Coat the fish with the butter/oil mixture so it's evenly coated.
3. Transfer the fish to the grill, cooking on each side for 4-5 minutes per side.
4. The fish is done when it flakes apart or it reaches 135-140° in the thickest part of the meat.
5. Use remaining sauce for dipping.

Serving Suggestion: Ginger couscous or cold pasta salad with herb biscuits.

Just for the Halibut

Halibut are native to the North Atlantic Ocean and the Gulf of Alaska. These huge fish often weigh in at 45-100 pounds. They're unique in that they swim horizontally, having a life span of about 45 years. It's an effective substitute for any recipe that calls for white fish. A 3.5 ounce halibut filet has only 110 calories, and you can store halibut in the freezer for up to 6 months.

Special Feature...

Whole Herbed Black Sea Bass

If you're looking for awe-struck faces, nothing makes a flashy presentation quite like a whole fish properly dressed. Black Sea Bass is a full-bodied, lean fish with a mild flavor. In any form, this fish tastes best when it has not been frozen.

Time: 15-20 minutes
Difficulty: ★★☆☆☆
Yield: Serves 3
Shelf Life: 2-3 days

Equipment

♦ Mixing Bowl
♦ Whisk or Spoon
♦ Sharp Knife
♦ Toothpick
♦ Grilling Tools

Ingredients

• 3 pounds scaled, cleaned Sea Bass
• Salt: Hawaiian smoked or Sesame
• 3 mandarin oranges, sliced
• Sprigs of dill, thyme, parsley and basil
• Sesame or olive oil

Directions

(PREP)

1. Rinse your sea bass.
2. Score both sides of the fish using a knife from head to tail.
3. Sprinkle it lightly with salt both inside and out.
4. Stuff the belly of the fish with the oranges and herb sprigs (reserve some of each for your presentation—how much you use is up to personal taste).
5. Lightly oil the fish skin.

(COOK)

1. Turn the grill to high heat so you can sear the fish's skin. Oil the grate liberally.
2. Place the fish on one side, with the tail of the fish farthest away from the hottest part of your grill (this section cooks more quickly than the rest.)
3. Watch for the skin to crisp up. This takes about 6 minutes, depending on the thickness of your fish. You're looking for opaque meat.
4. Gently turn the fish using a spatula. If it doesn't release, give it another minute or two.
5. If a toothpick easily slides through the thickest portion and/or the fish flakes easily, it's done (and don't worry if you find out it's not quite ready yet—a quick trip to the oven won't hurt a thing.)

Serving Suggestion: Grilled pepper salad or avocado salad, with Pinot Grigio pairing.

Shellfish

Like other types of fish, shellfish offer a low-fat alternative to other meats. Consider that shrimp have only one gram of fat in a per-person serving. All shellfish are low-cholesterol, high in protein, and rich in Omega-3 fatty acids. These support heart health, mental focus, and may even alleviate certain cognitive issues like depression and memory loss.

A vast majority of shellfish is cooked in the shell, which provides protection and helps keep the fish moist. When cooking out of the shell, you must monitor your barbecue closely to avoid rubbery, dry results.

Old Bay Mixed Grill

This mixed grill makes a great finger-style appetizer for nearly any cookout. When shopping for this recipe, remember to buy three extra of each type of shellfish as some will inevitably fail to open, and must be discarded.

Time: 5-10 minutes
Difficulty: ★★☆☆☆
Yield: Serves 3
Shelf Life: 2-3 days

Equipment

♦ Sauce Pan
♦ Food Scrubber
♦ Zester/Grater
♦ Heat-proof Bowl
♦ Sauce Containers (Shot Glasses or Sake cups)
♦ Grilling Tools

Ingredients

• 15 raw clams, oysters and mussels
• 3 Tbsp. filtered water
• 1 cup softened butter
• 1 Tbsp. Old Bay or Seafood Seasoning
• ½ Tbsp. finely grated red onion
• ½ Tbsp. finely grated garlic
• 1 tsp. grated lemon zest (optional)
• Fresh Parsley (garnish)

Directions

(PREP)

1. Put the water in your saucepan over medium heat.
2. When the water starts to simmer, turn the heat down to low.
3. Slowly add the softened butter, whisking it into the water.
4. The butter will begin getting creamy after you've whisked about 1/3 cup.
5. Continue adding the rest of the butter, slowly to maintain consistency.
6. Turn off the stove, stir in all the spices and let the sauce sit (this is the dipping sauce) while you prepare and cook the shellfish.
7. Scrub the shellfish in cold water, removing any sand and dirt. Pat dry.
8. Preheat your grill to medium-high.

(COOK)

1. Place the shellfish on the direct heat of the grill. Oysters should be cooked with the cup-side down.
2. Cover the grill.
3. Check the fish in about 5 minutes. Some of the mussels and oysters should be open and bubbly. Transfer these to a heat-proof bowl.
4. Close the lid again for another 3 minutes and the remaining mussels and oysters should be open, with juices sizzling. Add the cooked ones to your serving bowl. *continued...*

5. Close the lid again, waiting 2-3 more minutes. Large clams may take as long as 10 minutes to fully open, due to their size.
6. Discard any of the shellfish that do not open.
7. Use ½ of the cooked shell as a serving "dish". Each guest receives 4 of each type of shellfish.
8. Sprinkle bits of parsley evenly over the serving plate. Use sake cups or shot glasses for each guest filled with a little sauce so they can dip OR pour.

Serving Suggestion: Enjoy with kimchi and white wine.

TIP Buy similarly sized shellfish so that the cooking times won't vary as much. The average cooking time for clams is eight minutes, and mussels and oysters five minutes (depending on the size—larger shellfish take longer to pop open). Retain the shells and use them for making a rich shellfish broth.

Special Feature...

Lobster Legacy

In the 1600s, people at Plymouth Plantation were eating lobster that washed up onto the beaches in literal piles. There was so much of an abundance of this shellfish that it was considered a food suited to prisoners, poor people, and the "help" (sounds like a great time to be an indentured servant!)

In the 19th century, lobster came in a can like tuna and sold for 11 cents a pound. Some considered it perfect for a cat, and the cats probably heartily agreed. The advent of railways introduced lobster to travelers and new cities. By the mid-1800s, restaurants began serving lobster, and soon this distant cousin to the spider would be a global sensation, fetching prices that the Pilgrims could never have imagined.

Lobster Tails

Lobster is one of those foods of which I never tire. It's so rich and silky, and makes a wonderful main dish for celebratory occasions. This is a fairly standard and straight-forward approach to lobster as, in my opinion, this shellfish needs little in the way of adornment other than good butter. Note that rather than attempting to **butterfly** *the lobster yourself at home (which can lead to disappointing results if done improperly), ask your butcher to do so when you buy the tails. Use the tails as soon as possible afterward.*

Time: 10 minutes
Difficulty: ★☆☆☆☆
Yield: Serves 4
Shelf Life: 2-3 days

Equipment

♦ Mixing Bowl
♦ Whisk or Spoon
♦ Metal Skewers
♦ Pastry/Grilling Brush
♦ Grilling Tools

Ingredients

• (4) 6 oz. butterflied lobster tails
• ½ cup unsalted butter, softened
• 1 clove fresh garlic, finely minced
• 1 tsp. parsley
• 1 tsp. chives
• 1 tsp. fresh ground pepper
• Extra virgin olive oil
• Lemon

Directions

(PREP)
1. Preheat the grill to medium high heat.
2. Lightly rinse the lobster for any bits of sand or dirt.
3. Insert the metal skewer into the tail of the fish so it lays flat/straight (this makes for even cooking.)

(COOK)
1. Grill over direct heat with the exposed meat side down until the shell turns a vivid red (5 minutes).
2. Turn the lobster over and brush each tail evenly with some of the butter mixture.
3. Continue cooking until the lobster meat turns opaque (4 minutes).
4. Plate with herb butter for dipping sauce and lemon wedges.

Serving Suggestion: Pair with Caesar salad, garlic rolls and Champagne.

Shop Talk...

Butterfly; Verb. Cutting a meat halfway through the thickest part, and then opening it to lay flat. This method helps food cook more evenly.

Sassy Shrimp

There are over 2,000 types of shrimp in the world. Warm-water shrimp make up the vast majority of consumer fare, with black tiger shrimp the most commonly available in the market. These appetizer shrimp have a delicate flavor with a medium-to-firm texture, making them a great choice for your grill.

Time: 10 minutes
Difficulty: ★☆☆☆☆
Yield: Serves 4
Shelf Life: 2 days

Equipment

♦ Mixing Bowl
♦ Whisk or Spoon
♦ Food Storage Bag
♦ Skewers
♦ Basting Bowl and Brush
♦ Grilling Tools

Ingredients

• 1 pound large raw, tail-on shrimp (peeled and deveined)
• 1 cup white wine
• ⅛ cup fresh chopped parsley
• 2 cloves minced garlic
• 2 Tbsp. hot sauce (any type you like)
• 1 tsp. oregano
• 1 tsp. basil
• 1 tsp. black pepper
• **Pat of butter**

Directions

(PREP)

1. Mix everything except the shrimp and butter in a bowl.
2. Transfer this into a food storage bag, keeping about ¼ cup for basting.
3. Add your shrimp to the bag and seal.
4. Marinate in the refrigerator for 1-2 hours.
5. Preheat the grill for low-medium heat.
6. Place the shrimp on the skewers so that you pierce the head and tail.

(COOK)

1. Once it's hot, oil the grill grate.
2. Barbecue the shrimp on each side for 3 minutes, turning and using your reserved baste, then 2 minutes more each side. When the shrimp is opaque, it's cooked though.

Serving Suggestion: Minted peas or beans and pear wine.

Shop Talk...

Pat of butter; N. For many years, cooking writers did not give exact measurements for their recipes. This may have been a way to protect "secrets," or may have simply reflected common knowledge of that era. According to culinary experts, a pat of butter is roughly equivalent to ½ teaspoon.

Veggies and Tofu

More and more people are endeavoring to eat healthier. Additionally, numerous people have turned to veganism or vegetarianism as a mindful lifestyle choice. These changes do not mean that your grill has to sit cold. Fire it up and make some wonderful main and side dishes that have the unique barbecue flavor sans meat!

Cooking vegetables on the grill gives them a different flavor than the stove or oven. Just remember that soft, tender vegetables cook very quickly and become mushy if not watched carefully.

Whole Herbed Black Sea Bass

This medley can be made any time of year but somehow it reminds me of fall and the earth's abundance. You can change out the vegetables in any way you wish so long as the overall proportions remain the same (if you're cooking for three to four as a side dish.)

Time: 25 minutes
Difficulty: ★☆☆☆☆
Yield: Serves 3-4
Shelf Life: 3-4 days

Equipment

♦ Mixing Bowl
♦ Whisk or Spoon
♦ Food Storage Bag
♦ Small Sauce Dish
♦ Grilling Basket
♦ Grilling Tools

Ingredients

• ½ Cup olive oil
• ⅛ cup balsamic vinegar
• ⅛ cup white wine
• 1 tsp. parsley flakes
• 1 tsp. Italian seasoning blend
• ½ Tbsp. fresh minced garlic
• ½ tsp. each salt and pepper
• 1 sweet green pepper ½" slices
• 1 sweet orange pepper ½" slices
• ½ pound butternut squash ½" square pieces
• ½ pound zucchini ½" square pieces
• 12 button mushrooms
• ½ pound asparagus (trim off the hard ends)
• 6 green onions (or one red onion sliced ½" pieces)
• 6 baby purple potatoes halved
• 12 baby carrots

Directions

(PREP)

1. Mix the liquid and spices together in a large mixing bowl.
2. Set aside ¼ cup of the herb mixture for a finishing sauce.
3. Add your vegetables to the remaining herb blend and coat thoroughly.
4. Transfer the vegetables to a food storage bag and marinate for at least 1 hour before cooking.

(COOK)

1. Heat the grill to medium high, treating the grates with a little cooking oil.
2. Place potatoes and carrots in the basket for two minutes, followed by the green peppers, squash, and zucchini. Lastly, add the asparagus and onions.
3. Continue grilling for about 4-6 more minutes, tossing the vegetables until they show an even, lightly browned edge.

Serving Suggestion: Pair with Syrah and pita or naan bread.

TIP Add in the hardest vegetables like carrots and potatoes to the grilling basket first, followed by softer items like asparagus and mushrooms so that everything finishes at the same time without overcooking. Carrots and potatoes cook in about 9 minutes over medium high heat. Squash and mushrooms take about 7 minutes and green onions and asparagus a mere four minutes.

Grilled Tofu

This medley can be made any time of year but somehow it reminds me of fall and the earth's abundance. You can change out the vegetables in any way you wish so long as the overall proportions remain the same (if you're cooking for three to four as a side dish.)

Time: 15 minutes
Difficulty: ★★☆☆☆
Yield: Serves 4
Shelf Life: 3-5 days

Equipment
♦ Mixing Bowl
♦ Whisk or Spoon
♦ 2 Plates
♦ A Brick*
♦ Knife
♦ Rectangular Baking Pan
♦ Skewers
♦ Grilling Tools

*Or any item weighing about 4 pounds that fits on top of a plate.

Ingredients
• 14. oz. firm tofu
• ¼ cup soy sauce
• 1 Tbsp. lemon juice
• 1 Tbsp. rice wine vinegar
• 1 Tbsp. sesame oil
• 1 Tbsp. minced garlic
• 1 tsp. red pepper flakes
• 1 Tbsp. brown sugar

Directions

(PREP)
1. Drain the tofu and place on a plate with a second plate on top (inverted.)
2. Put the weight on the plate and leave it for a half hour.
3. Drain the liquid pressed from the tofu.
4. Section into four equal sized parts.   *continued...*

5. Mix the marinade.
6. Pour half the marinade in the bottom of the baking pan.
7. Lay the tofu in the pan. Pour the remaining marinade over top.
8. Refrigerate for 2 hours prior to cooking.

(COOK)
1. Preheat the grill to medium (325°.)
2. Drain and skewer the tofu. Grill each side for 3 minutes, then turn and brush with marinade. Repeat this three more times so each side receives about 6 minutes of grilling.

Serving Suggestion:Enjoy with a tomato cucumber salad or fresh corn on the cob.

TIP Use extra firm tofu on the grill so it doesn't fall apart, and bear in mind that grilling tofu on a stick is more manageable than using tongs (which can make the tofu fall apart.) You can choose any marinade for tofu, whether you make it yourself or buy it at the supermarket, though pre-seasoned tofu makes a fun alternative to marinating.

Crispy Potatoes

I often make this dish indoors in the winter. Come the heat of summer, however, I transfer my potatoes to the grill to get that great crisp (and to keep my kitchen cool!)

Time: 15 minutes
Difficulty: ★☆☆☆☆
Yield: Serves 2
Shelf Life: 5-7 days

Equipment
♦ Mixing Bowl
♦ Whisk or Spoon
♦ Toothpick
♦ Grilling Tools

Ingredients
• 2 Russet potatoes, scrubbed
• 2 Tbsp. vegetable oil
• ½ tsp. each salt and pepper
• ½ tsp. malt vinegar
• ¼ tsp onion powder
• ¼ tsp. garlic powder
• ¼ tsp. dill
• Sea salt

Directions

(PREP)

1. Slice the potatoes in 1/4" thick slices.
2. Mix the oil and spices, except the sea salt.
3. Preheat the grill to medium high.
4. Brush the grill grates with oil.

(COOK)

1. Put the slices of potato directly on the grill.
2. In about 6 minutes, or when one side is lightly browned turn the potatoes with a spatula (NOT tongs.)
3. Brush the upward side of the potatoes with oil and spices.
4. Turn the potatoes again after about 6 minutes (or until the other side browns.)
5. Brush the 2nd side of the potatoes with the oil mix.
6. Reduce your grill temperature to medium. Cook about another 7 minutes until tender all the way thru (use a toothpick to test.)
7. Sprinkle lightly with sea salt just before serving.

Serving Suggestion: Grilled green beans (Hericots Verts or Long style;) pair with a sweeter Chardonnay.

Sumptuous Sides

Side dishes are the fringe on the barbecue table cloth. We often think in terms of barbecuing just our main dish, but why not use that heat for your side dishes too? It takes a little bit of space planning and good timing, but it saves energy and opens up opportunities for new twists on old favorites.

KEY POINT *Side dishes can become a highlight of your meal by using a little creativity and planning your grill space accordingly.*

Grilled Corn Salad

This is an easy, healthy salad that you can enjoy hot or cold. If you plan to serve it hot, I suggest grilling the tomatoes, peppers, and scallions, too. Otherwise, pre-prepare the cold salad and top it with warm corn.

Time: 7 minutes
Difficulty: ★☆☆☆☆
Yield: Serves 5
Shelf Life: 4 days

Equipment

♦ Salad Bowl
♦ Mixing Bowl
♦ Whisk or Spoon
♦ Small Sauce Bowl
♦ Knife
♦ Grilling Tools

Ingredients

• 5 ears of corn, husked
• 2 Tbsp. vegetable oil
• Fresh ground salt & pepper
• 1 ½ cup grape tomatoes, halved
• 3 minced scallions
• ¾ medium sweet orange pepper, sliced ¼" pieces
• 2 limes, juiced
• ¼ cup olive oil
• 2 cloves garlic, minced
• 1 Tbsp. smoky paprika
• 1 tsp. onion powder
• 1 tsp. basil
• ¼ cup sugar
• Feta crumbles (optional)

Directions

(PREP)

1. Preheat the barbecue to medium.
2. Brush each ear of corn with vegetable oil and sprinkle a little salt and pepper on all sides.
3. Place the tomatoes, scallions and pepper in a salad bowl.
4. Mix all the remaining ingredients together and put them in a sauce bowl—this is your salad dressing.

(COOK)

1. Grill the corn for about 7 minutes, turning regularly for evenness. It should be lightly brown.
2. When the corn reaches room temperature, remove it from ear with a knife.
3. Add to the rest of the salad and toss with dressing.
4. Add feta crumbles for garnish if desired.

Serving Suggestion: This is tasty with crab or skirt steak and Sauvignon Blanc.

Figs in Bacon

Warning: these are addictive. They benefit from the addition of smoking wood if you want (apple is a nice choice) and don't forget that figs are not the only thing you can wrap in bacon! I also like stuffing with honey-seasoned ground meat, walnuts, and chutney, to name a few.

Time: 10 minutes
Difficulty: ★★☆☆☆
Yield: Serves 4-5
Shelf Life: 2-3 days

Ingredients
- 20 dried figs
- 10 slices of bacon
- 4 oz. goat cheese, softened
- 3 Tbsp. aged balsamic vinegar
- 3 Tbsp. honey

Equipment
♦ Knife
♦ Small Spoon
♦ Baking Pan
♦ Sauce Pan
♦ Toothpicks
♦ Tongs
♦ Grilling Basket
♦ Grilling Tools

Directions

(PREP)

1. Using your knife, make a slit into the side of each fig (this acts like a pocket).
2. Stuff about 1 tsp. of goat cheese into each fig. Set aside.   *continued...*

(COOK)

1. Preheat oven to 400 degrees.
2. Place the bacon on a baking sheet and cook about 4 minutes, then flip. Continue cooking until it is HALFWAY DONE (8-10 minutes total.) Remove from heat and let cool.
3. Combine vinegar and honey in a sauce pan and warm it up. This is a finishing sauce.
4. Slice the bacon in half (lengthwise.)
5. Wrap one piece around each fig's pocket, securing it in place with a toothpick.
6. Heat the grill to medium high.
7. Lightly oil the grilling basket and transfer the figs to it.
8. Grill for about 6 minutes, turning the figs so that the bacon finishes cooking up crisp.
9. Serve drizzled with the honey vinegar sauce.

Serving Suggestion: Mesclun salad and Chenin Blanc or rosé wine.

Grilled Naan

Any meal benefits from good, fresh bread. Naan, a kissing cousin to pita, is a staple of Indian foods. However, an unflavored bread element like this one suits any dish. It fluffs up quickly on a grill, so the biggest part of the work is preparing the dough.

Time: 10 minutes
Difficulty: ★★★☆☆
Yield: Serves 7
Shelf Life: 5 days

Equipment

♦ Mixing Bowls
♦ Cooking Tray
♦ Towel
♦ Rolling Pin
♦ Grilling Tools

Ingredients

• 1 package active dry yeast
• 1 cup warm water
• 3 Tbsp. sugar
• 3 Tbsp. plain yogurt
• 1 Tbsp. vegetable oil
• 2 tsp. salt
• 4 cups bread flour
• ¼ cup butter, melted
• Oil and flour

Directions

(PREP)

1. Pour the yeast into the cup of warm (NOT HOT) water, along with the sugar.

2. Leave this to sit for 15 minutes until very frothy, then combine with flour, yogurt, oil and salt in a large mixing bowl.
3. Knead by hand for about 7 minutes until the dough forms. Transfer ball of dough to an oiled mixing bowl. Cover it with a clean, damp towel in a warm location.
4. Let the dough rise for 1 hour (it should double in volume).
5. Separate dough into 7 equal size pieces, rolling them into balls.
6. Put these on a tray covered with a towel for a half hour. They should double in size.
7. Flour a cutting board and roll out the dough into a roughly circular shape.
8. Lightly oil your barbecue grates.
9. Preheat your grill to high heat.

(COOK)
1. Transfer each piece of Naan to the grill. Cook for 3 minutes, brushing the upward side with butter.
2. Turn and brush again, waiting another 3 minutes. When the Naan is lightly browned, it's ready to come off the grill (note that you may need to turn it again.)

Serving Suggestion: Serve with an olive oil dipping sauce or with a traditional Tzatziki sauce.

TIP
You can add all manner of spices to naan (two tsp. total for this portion size). Suggestions include garlic and basil with butter for a savory flavor, or ginger and cinnamon (and dipped in honey after cooking) for a sweet version. If you don't consider yourself much a baker (like me), you can buy Naan at many supermarkets. It comes in many varieties including white, whole wheat and garlic. I like the Stonefire brand.

Shop Talk...

Tzatziki; N. Greek cold sauce, often used as a dip, made from yogurt, cucumbers, olive oil and garlic. Some common additions include parsley, dill and mint.

Picnic Fare, Pot Lucks and Beach Bonfires

Inevitably, you'll be making barbecue for on-the-go events. Be it a private picnic with a partner, a pot luck at church or food for a beach bonfire, you'll need dishes that easily transport from one place to the next, and that you can properly store en route for food safety. Here are a few of my favorites.

Fajitas

This recipe has a great Tex-mex flavor profile. Fajitas are easy to make on the spot, or you can pre-make the meat and fillings and warm everything up when you reach your destination.

Time: 25 minutes
Difficulty: ★★☆☆☆
Yield: Serves 4-5
Shelf Life: 3-4 days

Equipment
♦ Mixing Bowl
♦ Whisk or Spoon
♦ Baking Pan
♦ Skewers
♦ Grilling Tools
♦ Cutting Board and Knife

Ingredients
• 1/4 cup chopped fresh cilantro
• 1 cup olive oil
• 1 cup Tequila
• 3 Tbsp. lime juice
• 1 tsp. cumin
• ½ tsp chili powder
• 1 clove garlic minced
• ½ tsp. salt and pepper
• 1 pound chicken breast or beef steak
• 4 lemon dip peppers*
• 2 orange sweet peppers
• 1 large red onion
• Oil, salt and pepper

Alternatively, Hungarian hot peppers or Chipotle for smokiness

Directions

(PREP)
1. Mix cilantro, oil, juice and spices together. Set aside half of this for basting.
2. Put your beef or chicken into a baking pan and pour the remaining marinade over the top. Let this sit in the refrigerator for one hour.
3. In the meantime, cut the small peppers in half and quarter the onion, separating the layers.
4. Put the peppers and onion on the skewers, alternating them.

(COOK)
1. Bring the grill to medium heat, treating the grates with oil.
2. Grill the chicken or beef for about 7 minutes per side, basting with the tequila mix.

3. Put the vegetable skewers on at the same time, as they need about 15 minutes. Turn them for even tenderness, basting as you go.
4. Transfer the meat to a cutting board and when rested for 10 minutes, slice into strips.
5. Put the meat into an airtight container for travel, as well as the baste and vegetables.

Serving Suggestion: Serve with tomato salsa, sour cream and guacamole.

 Do not pre-fill and wrap your soft tortillas before your outdoor adventure. They will get soggy en route.

Grilled Blossoming Onion

This is such a pretty dish. Use small red, yellow and white onions and serve as a per-person dish, or make HUGE onions and get everyone in on the pulling-dipping-eating fun. Since it's not deep fried, it's healthy too!

Time: 30 minutes
Difficulty: ★☆☆☆☆
Yield: Serves 1 per onion
Shelf Life: 3-4 days

Equipment
♦ Knife
♦ Aluminum Foil
♦ Bowl of Ice Water
♦ Smoking Wood (optional)

Ingredients
• 1 small red, white or yellow onion per person
• 2 Tbs. powdered Parmesan and Romano cheese
• ¼ Tbsp. Olive oil
• ½ tsp. garlic powder
• ¼ tsp red pepper powder
• Salt and pepper

Directions

(PREP)
1. Cut the onions into six equal sized wedges without cutting through the bottom.
2. Put the onions into the ice water for 10 minutes. This helps separate the "petals."
3. Drain on a paper towel, then use your fingers to open the wedges a little more (be careful; you don't want to separate them from the bottom).

4. Mix together dry spices.
5. Evenly coat the onion with olive oil, then sprinkle with the spices, endeavoring to give each petal a little bit of the blend.

(COOK)
1. Preheat the grill to medium high.
2. If you are planning to smoke the onions, start your smoking wood now.
3. Wrap each onion in aluminum foil.
4. Grill with the flat bottom down for 25 minutes. Open the wrap a little for the last 5-10 minutes so the onion absorbs the smoke aroma and flavor.
5. Note: you can remove the onion from the aluminum and put it on the fire if you like it more caramelized.

Serving Suggestion: Enjoy with steak sauce or spicy mayo—I serve mine with a sauce made of 2/3 tsp. smoky paprika, 3-4 Tbsp. horseradish sauce, 2 Tbsp. ketchup and a cup of mayo or white salad dressing. YUM. For a pretty presentation, place each onion on a bed of curly leaf lettuce.

TIP Unpeeled onions last for 1-2 months in the refrigerator before showing signs of bruising. Peeled onions last only a week. You can extend the shelf life by wrapping them in a paper towel before putting them in the vegetable bin.

Greek Lamb Kabobs

For a taste of the old world that transports you to the cliffs of Santorini overlooking sparkling blue waters at sunset, just take a bite of these lamb kabobs. So tender and juicy!

Time: 15 minutes
Difficulty: ★★☆☆☆
Yield: Serves 1 per onion
Shelf Life: 3-4 days

Equipment

♦ Mixing Bowls (2)
♦ Whisk or Spoon
♦ Skewers
♦ Grilling Tools

Ingredients

• 2 pounds of cubed lamb (1/2")
• 2 cloves minced garlic
• 2 tsp. Greek oregano
• 1 tsp. each ground salt and pepper
• 1 tsp. parley
• ½ tsp. ground thyme
• 1 tsp paprika
• 1 tsp. marjoram
• 3 Tbsp. red wine vinegar
• 3 Tbsp. olive oil
• Greek Yogurt
• Pita

Directions

(PREP)

1. Place the lamb cubes in a large mixing bowl.
2. Blend together all the remaining ingredients in a second small bowl. Stir until well integrated.
3. Pour this over the lamb, and stir thoroughly until all sides of the cubes are coated. Let marinate for 2 hours in the refrigerator. Hint: if you are going to serve this with a tomato cucumber salad, this is the perfect time to prepare it.

(COOK)

1. Turn the grill on for medium-high heat, treating the grates lightly with oil.
6. Skewer the lamb, putting about 5 pieces per skewer.
7. Put these on the grill, letting each side cook for 4 minutes. You are looking for an internal temperature of about 150-160 (medium). Don't overcook them!
8. Warm the pita on the grill.
9. Place a heaping teaspoon in the middle of each pita. Spread that up and down to make a line into which you'll "nest" the lamb.
10. Add the lamb and dress with some type of Greek condiment.

Serving Suggestion: A tomato orzo salad on the side; mint cucumber sauce for dipping.

Special Feature...

Barbecue Lemon-Limeade

Ok—I wasn't going to let you close this book without a surprise ending. Namely, a grilled beverage to accompany your outdoor adventures. What a refreshing drink, and so traditional to barbecue events!

Begin with 8 lemons and 12 limes. Wash them, then cut them in half. Dip the exposed fruit end of the lemon and limes in a blend of white and Hawaiian sugar (if you only have white sugar that's fine). Transfer these face down to a lightly oiled, very clean (no residue) grill heated to 325o. In about five minutes, the sugar begins caramelizing. Take care not to let the fruit blacken. Remove them and cool.

While they cool, make a syrup of honey and water using ½ cup of honey to 2 cups water. Simmer until mixed. Pour this into a pitcher, adding another 5 cups of water (so it reaches the ½ gallon mark). Squeeze the lemons and limes into the mix. Taste and adjust for sweetness.

Move to the refrigerator. Serve cold over ice with a hint of bourbon or whiskey.

TIP If you need greater sweetness, pour off a little liquid into a sauce pan and add either sugar or honey to it. Dissolve and return it to the container (otherwise the sweetener tends to sink to the bottom). Make your ice out of some commercial lemonade. This way your beverage won't get watery as the ice melts.

THE TAKEAWAY

▶ Basic barbecue sauce consists of a sugar, an acid and a foundation like ketchup to which cooks add a variety of spices based on personal taste and experience. The best barbecue sauces are those that stick to the main component and don't overwhelm any other flavors in your meal.

▶ Both sweet and savory sauces serve a purpose in great barbecue. They give you ways of changing up your flavors while using a base that's still familiar and accommodating. Don't be afraid to mix the two from time to time and see what "secret" recipe you create!

▶ As you explore barbecue sauces from around the world you'll also have an opportunity to expose your taste buds to all kinds of herbs and spices, some of which you may have never even heard of. As you do, remember that food is a deep reflection of a people's culture, beliefs, and traditions.

▶ Creative use of color makes for pleasing barbecue presentations. In this case, you get both color and rich flavor.

▶ Finishing sauces can be a traditional barbecue sauce applied at the end of cooking, or drizzled over top of a component prior to serving. They can also be wholly different creations that match your meal's flavor profile.

▶ While a recipe may call for ground beef, you can substitute any other ground product you choose including game meats. Just remember to check internal temperature guidelines to insure that your food is cooked safely.

▶ Chicken is perhaps the most adaptable meat you'll ever "meet." It accepts flavors readily, making it an ideal background for outstanding barbecue sauces and rubs.

▶ Pork is a carbohydrate-free meat – so get rid of the guilt and grab a napkin!

▶ Firm fish is better for barbecuing. If you use a more delicate fish like tilapia it's best to use a non-stick fish grilling basket, which you can find at most department stores with the other barbecue equipment.

▶ A vast majority of shellfish is cooked in the shell, which provides protection and helps keep the fish moist. When cooking out of the shell, you must monitor your barbecue closely to avoid rubbery, dry results.

▶ Cooking vegetables on the grill gives them a different flavor than the stove or oven. Just remember that soft, tender vegetables cook very quickly and become mushy if not watched carefully.

▶ Side dishes can become a highlight of your meal by using a little creativity and planning your grill space accordingly.

"There is no real need for decorations when throwing a barbecue party—let the summer garden, in all its vibrant and luscious splendor, speak for itself."

—Pippa Middleton, English socialite and author

The Wrap

That, as they say, is a wrap. Now you have a beginner-level knowledge of barbecue and grilling, all wrapped up in an oversized package. Bear in mind that *Grilling for Beginners* will always be here in your library of cookbooks to help you when you get stuck for ideas or techniques, but your real education will come from experience. No one becomes a pit master overnight!

Remember the suggestion at the beginning of the book—try to learn one recipe or method to the point where you're really confident, then go on to another. Each approach teaches you something new and expands your knowledge of this culinary art. Just one caution: I have found that barbecue is highly addictive—not only for the cook, but for all your hungry eaters. You'll get a lot of requests and find yourself wanting to pull out the grill, even in the middle of a snow storm.

Hey—why not? You now have all the knowledge you need to barbecue—or grill—come rain or shine, sleet or snow, any time of day or season of the year. Thanks for reading *Grilling for Beginners*! I wish you all the best—and hope that soon after you close this book, you find innumerable cherished memories, new traditions and delicious, unforgettable experiences rising around your bountiful table like a beautiful cloud of barbecue smoke.

I hope you've enjoyed this exploration, and that you develop the same passion for outdoor cuisine that I have.

May your fires always burn brightly!

Quick Reference Guide

For your convenience, here is a list of all the key points in the book:

1. Becoming a Grilling Guru

- Barbecue is a slow process that uses indirect heat and smoke to cook and flavor food, often large or tough cuts.
- Grilling is a fast, hot process suited for more delicate foods, or those items whose flavors benefit from direct flame.

2. Choosing a Grill

- Gas grills rule the consumer market because they're easy and offer even cooking temperatures.
- Size, shape and materials are three important keys to selecting the right grill for your home and lifestyle.
- No matter the grill, cleaning and maintaining it properly is essential for food safety and the longevity of your unit.
- Charcoal is unpredictable compared to gas but it imparts a distinct flavor and aroma to your food.
- Wood imparts great flavor, and having a barbecue pit as part of the landscape is an easy way to bring a social element to your backyard.

3. Have Pot Holder, Will Travel

- Select your tools of the trade wisely. This improves your overall success and safety.
- Pick a cutting board for your barbecue that suits the type of food you're serving. Use wood for bread and vegetables, and plastic for meats.
- Always use hand protection when working your grill. This is a matter of safety, as is having a functional fire extinguisher and accurate thermometer.
- For reaching, moving, and serving food, use long tools with comfortable handles.
- Wood choices for smoked dishes should reflect the recipe and the delicateness or robustness of the main offering.

4. Getting Ready

- Safety first: When in doub—throw it out.
- Good planning and preparation creates a much more relaxed atmosphere whether you're cooking for family or a whole slew of guests.
- Temperature affects food safety both in the way you store an item and the internal temperature to which you cook each component.
- Proper methods for defrosting, marinating, and packing your barbecue ingredients on ice help keep the food safe from bacteria.
- Cook smaller portions based on the order of your meal. You can pay closer attention to the food and keep the remaining portions chilling until you need them.

5. Marvelous Marinades and Rubs

- Use the best fresh or dried spices you can find for your marinades and rubs. Remember to add them slowly, tasting as you go.
- The herbs in commercial or homemade rubs can easily transform into a marinade simply by adding a liquid base.
- Experimentation is part of the learning process. Write down your successes for future reference.
- For flexibility work with chicken.
- Paprika is the most common spice used in barbecue rubs
- Many of the spice blends for chicken work well on fish too.
- Soft vegetables accept flavor from marinade, but harder vegetables or vegetable powder can go into your blend for greater flavor.

6. Smoking Hot Ideas

- Brines and mops are good methods for keeping meat moist during the smoking process.
- Always use food-grade wood for smoking food. Do not use any wood of which you do not know the source.
- Use strong, heady woods on similarly strong flavored foods.
- Endeavor to use an electric or natural source for starting your wood on fire.
- It is not necessary to soak your smoking wood.
- Keep it low and slow, opening the unit as little as possible throughout the cooking process.

7. Fresh from the Rotisserie

- Rotisseries create barbecue-like flavor at reasonable prices.
- Like a barbecue grill, the origin of the rotisserie is lost to history, but it remains an excellent addition to barbecue efforts.
- Shop around to find a rotisserie that's large enough for your family and entertaining needs and has all the features you want.
- Rotisserie cooking isn't hard and it keeps your main dish moist and flavorful.
- The keys to great rotisserie recipes are a balanced skewer, good seasoning blends, the right temperature and timing.

8. History, Mystery and Myth

- The discovery and control of fire revolutionized human civilization and advanced human development in significant ways.
- The folklore and superstitions surrounding fire reflect early humankind's reverence toward this element, and provide cultural peeks into how early people explained fire's creation.

9. Recipes

- Basic barbecue sauce consists of a sugar, an acid and a foundation like ketchup to which cooks add a variety of spices based on personal taste and experience. The best barbecue sauces are those that stick to the main component and don't overwhelm any other flavors in your meal.

- Both sweet and savory sauces serve a purpose in great barbecue. They give you ways of changing up your flavors while using a base that's still familiar and accommodating. Don't be afraid to mix the two from time to time and see what "secret" recipe you create!

- As you explore barbecue sauces from around the world you'll also have an opportunity to expose your taste buds to all kinds of herbs and spices, some of which you may have never even heard of. As you do, remember that food is a deep reflection of a people's culture, beliefs, and traditions.

- Creative use of color makes for pleasing barbecue presentations. In this case, you get both color and rich flavor.

- Finishing sauces can be a traditional barbecue sauce applied at the end of cooking, or drizzled over top of a component prior to serving. They can also be wholly different creations that match your meal's flavor profile.

- While a recipe may call for ground beef, you can substitute any other ground product you choose including game meats. Just remember to check internal temperature guidelines to insure that your food is cooked safely.

- Chicken is perhaps the most adaptable meat you'll ever "meet." It accepts flavors readily, making it an ideal background for outstanding barbecue sauces and rubs.

- Pork is a carbohydrate-free meat—so get rid of the guilt and grab a napkin!

- Firm fish is better for barbecuing. If you use a more delicate fish like tilapia it's best to use a non-stick fish grilling basket, which you can find at most department stores with the other barbecue equipment.

- A vast majority of shellfish is cooked in the shell, which provides protection and helps keep the fish moist. When cooking out of the shell, you must monitor your barbecue closely to avoid rubbery, dry results.

- Cooking vegetables on the grill gives them a different flavor than the stove or oven. Just remember that soft, tender vegetables cook very quickly and become mushy if not watched carefully.

- Side dishes can become a highlight of your meal by using a little creativity and planning your grill space accordingly.

Bet you didn't realize until you saw that list just how much you've already learned! If you stick with these key points, you'll find that your ongoing adventure with barbecue is ultimately safe, succulent, and successful. But don't stop here! As you experiment, write down other things that you discover, want to avoid or, hopefully, use again and again. Share your ideas with other grillers, unless you want to keep your secrets to amaze and amuse (or maybe someday write a book for beginners)— but at the very least, you've got to share them with me!

The Deep Dish

The Deep Dish is a section for you go-getters who want to continue your education beyond the confines of this mere tome. Here are my recommendations for other great resources:

BOOKS

Barbecue: a Global History; Jonathan Deutsch and Megan Elias; 2014. *A tidy, 144-page book that shares the ancient roots of barbecue and continues the story up to modern day competitions.*

Barbecue: A History of an American Institution; Robert Moss; 2013. *A book that recounts the growth of barbecue—from Native American methods to what became a social cornerstone in the United States.*

The Barbecue Bible; Steven Raichlen; 2008. *This award winning best seller is a MUST for your barbecue collection. If 500 recipes weren't enough, there's full colored images and guidance for beginner and adept alike.*

Barbecue Bible Sauces, Rubs, and Marinades; Bastes, Butters and Glazes; Steven Raichlen; 2000. *A great companion to the Barbecue Bible that expands your portfolio with both classic and innovative selections. 200+ recipes.*

Cooks Illustrated Guide to Grilling and Barbecue: Cooks Illustrated Magazine Editors; 2005. *Grilling essentials, outdoor buying guide, and 452 recipes from a well-trusted culinary magazine.*

Essential New York Times Grilling Cookbook: More than 100 Years of Sizzling Food Writing and Recipes; Peter Kaminsky and Mark Bittman; 2014. *A collection of New York Times barbecue and grilling articles along with savory recipes and a little storytelling on the side.*

Food in History; Reay Tannahill; 1995. A staple in my collection. *While not specifically about barbecue, it's a great insight into how food influenced life around the world.*

Guy on Fire: 130 Recipe for Adventures in Outdoor Cooking; Guy Fieri; 2014. *The notable Food Network chef takes us on an adventure in outdoor cooking, from simple campfires to backyard grills.*

Marinades, Rubs, Brines, Cures and Glazes; Jim Tarantino; 2006. *400 recipes to make any meal sweet, spicy or savory. A great way to build your repertoire.*

The Deep Dish

Much Depends on Dinner: The Extraordinary History and Mythology, Allure and Obsessions, Perils and Taboos of an Ordinary Meal. Margaret Visser; 2010. *Another book that's not specifically about grilling, but offers a great look at the history of our food, and why we cook and present the way we do.*

Rotisserie Grilling: 50 Recipes for your Grill's Rotisserie; Mike Vrobel; 2012. *Whether you're just starting out or already hooked on rotisserie cooking, this book gives you some wonderful recipes that are tasty, but not overly ambitious.*

Smokin' with Myron Mixon: Recipes Made Simple from the Winningest Man in Barbecue; Myron Mixon; 2011. *Myron Mixon has been smoking food since he was a boy. He's won over 180 grand championships, and applies his know-how to this book, turning his attention to backyard grilling and barbecue (and how to keep it simple).*

The Ultimate Guide to America's Four Regional Styles of Cue; Dotty Griffith; 2002. *An exploration of Carolina, Memphis, Texas and Kansas City barbecue with authentic recipes.*

ONLINE

5@5 Busting Barbecue Myths: http://eatocracy.cnn.com/2013/04/01/55-busting-barbecue-myths/; 2014. *A great site produced by the CNN and Eatocracy crew with information on all things "foodie".*

Allrecipes Barbecue Sauces, Marinades and Rubs: http://allrecipes.com/recipes/bbq--grilling/bbq-sauces-marinades-and-rubs/. *This site is an excellent source for all kinds of recipes - even those that go back into the house.*

Amazing Ribs: http://amazingribs.com/; 2014. *This site is jam-packed with a ton of great grilling and barbecue information, including grill set ups, how to get grill flavor indoors, barbecue associations, barbecue myths and tools, just to name a few. Highly recommended.*

Barbecue and Food Safety: http://www.fsis.usda.gov/wps/portal/fsis/topics/food-safety-education/get-answers/food-safety-fact-sheets/safe-food-handling/barbecue-and-food-safety/ct_index; 2014. *A fact sheet on food safety when grilling, produced by the USDA Food Safety and Inspection Service.*

Barbecues Beginnings: http://news.harvard.edu/gazette/story/2012/04/barbecues-beginnings/; Steven Raichlen; 2012. *A brief but interesting takeaway from a lecture provided at Harvard by author Steven Raichlen.*

The Deep Dish

<u>Barbecue Pit Boys</u>: http://bbqpitboys.com/; 2014. *Great tips and tricks direct from these well-known pit masters, including how to create your own local Pit Master chapter.*

<u>BBQ—a Southern Cultural Icon</u>: http://xroads.virginia.edu/~CLASS/MA95/ dove/bbq.html; Laura Dove; 2014. *The history of barbecue in the South, including regional variations and recipes.*

<u>Barbecue State of Mind</u>: http://www.utexas.edu/features/2009/07/27/barbecue/; Jessica Sinn; 2014. *An engaging peek into Texas barbecue culture.*

<u>Brief History of Fire and its Uses</u>: http://hearth.com/what/historyfire.html; Ed Semmelroth; 2014. *A short piece that gives you a glimpse into the importance of fire to the ancients.*

<u>Cooking Channel</u>: http://www.cookingchanneltv.com/topics/barbecue. html/; 2014. *The site offers filters for your recipe searches, along with barbecue videos and helpful hints.*

<u>Cooking with Herbs and Spices</u>: http://www4.ncsu.edu/~aibrantl/cookingwithherbs.html; Ivy Reid; 2014. *A concise guide to pairing, using and storing herbs with several recipes for blends.*

<u>Fire</u>: http://www.mythencyclopedia.com/Dr-Fi/Fire.html; 2014. *A look into the myths behind the fire element from the Myth Encyclopedia.*

<u>Food Lab</u>: 7 Myths about Cooking Steak that Need to Go Away: http://www. seriouseats.com/2013/06/the-food-lab-7-old-wives-tales-about-cooking-steak. html; J. Kenji López-Alt; 2014. *Brought to you by Serious Eats, this article bust the myths that have haunted steak makers for years.*

<u>Food Network Grilling Central</u>; http://www.foodnetwork.com/grilling/grilling-central-barbecue.html. 2014. *Get recipes, tips and tricks from some of your favorite Food Network Stars.*

<u>General Grilling Safety</u>: http://www.hpba.org/consumers/barbecue/general-grilling-safety; 2014. Written by the Hearth, Patio and Barbecue Association. *Site includes popular accessories, grill feature consideration and interesting barbecue facts.*

<u>Grilling.Com</u>: http://www.grilling.com/; 2014. *A site designed by Kingsford, offers recipes, event information, techniques and blogs for the enthusiastic griller.*

The Deep Dish

<u>Grilling Safety Tips</u>: http://www.nfpa.org/safety-information/for-consumers/outdoors/grilling/grilling-safety-tips; 2014. *A website produced by the National Fire Prevention Organization with straight-forward ways to avoid barbecue fires.*

<u>Healthy Grilling Recipes</u>: http://www.eatingwell.com/recipes_menus/collections/healthy_grilling_recipes; 2014. *Far more than just a recipe site, Healthy Grilling comes to us from Eating Well where you can find healthy menu plans, blogs and much more.*

<u>Herbs Spices and Seasonings</u>: http://www.d.umn.edu/~alphanu/cookery/herbs.html; 2014. *Handy list assembled by the University of Minnesota, complete with flavor profiles (worth printing out and keeping in your spice cupboard.)*

<u>History of Fire Milestone</u>: http://www.huffingtonpost.com/2012/04/02/history-fire-million-homo-erectus_n_1397810.html; Charles Choi; 2014. *Archaeology shows us more about the controlled use of fire.*

<u>How to make Vegetables taste Better with Herbs and Spices</u>: http://www.streetdirectory.com/food_editorials/cooking/herbs_and_spices/how_to_make_vegetables_taste_better_with_herbs_and_spices.html; Deborah Prosser; 2014. *A great article on the effective use of herbs and spices with vegetables, and links to other culinary information.*

<u>International Barbecue Cookers Association</u>: http://ibcabbq.org/; 2014. *A group dedicated to providing networking and information on competitive barbecuing.*

<u>National Barbecue Association</u>: http://www.nbbqa.org/i4a/pages/index.cfm?pageid=1; 2014. *When you're ready to kick it up a notch, you can join a group like this and stay informed on what's new and great in the barbecue world.*

<u>National Barbecue News</u>: http://barbecuenews.com/calendar/; 2014. *This site offers a regularly updated calendar of events, along with barbecue forums, recipes and restaurants.*

<u>The Smoke Ring</u>: http://www.thesmokering.com/; 2014. *Links to over 1,000 barbecue websites.*

The Deep Dish

INGREDIENT SOURCES

♦ **Amazon.com**: http://www.amazon.com/s/ref=nb_sb_noss_1?url=-search-alias%3Daps&field-keywords=barbecue%20supplies&sprefix=bar-becue+su%2Caps; *A little bit of everything!*

♦ **BBQ Guys**: http://www.amazon.com/s/ref=nb_sb_noss_1?url=-search-alias%3Daps&field-keywords=barbecue%20supplies&sprefix=bar-becue+su%2Caps; *Gadgets and accessories.*

♦ **Far Away Foods:** http://www.farawayfoods.com/; *Not all barbecue related but you can find some unusual products here at reasonable prices.*

♦ **Grill Store and More**: http://www.thegrillstoreandmore.com/; *Wide range of specialty outdoor products including those suitable for barbecue cooking and entertaining.*

♦ **Goldbely**: https://www.goldbely.com/foods/tastes/bbq; *Meat, sauces and rubs.*

♦ **NutriFruit**: http://www.nutrifruit.com/; *Dehydrated fruit powder suited for rubs and marinade.*

♦ **Saltworks**: http://www.saltworks.us/gourmet-sea-salt.asp?g-clid=CNC_m-nmkMACFYMF7Aodkx4AHw; *Gourmet salt.*

♦ **San Francisco Herb Company**: http://www.sfherb.com/; *Bulk herbs, spices, teas, nuts and blends.*

♦ **Spice Barn**: http://www.spicebarn.com/?gclid=CPj82LbnkMACFSh-p7Aody1cANg; *One of my favorite spots for spices and herbs including rugs. Variety of sizes in packaging.*

The Lingo

Here, you'll find a glossary of all the Shop Talk terms used in the book.

- **Agave**—A sugar substitute that is also a chief component in tequila

- **Apple Slaw**—Shredded apples and other vegetables combined with mayonnaise and a variety of other ingredients

- **Brine**—A very strong saltwater that can serve as an alternative to marinade

- **Brown Sauce**—A British condiment similar to steak sauce

- **Butterfly**—A method of slicing meat halfway through its thickest section and laying the halves flat to ensure even cooking

- **Ceviche**—A method of curing raw fish with citric acid, hot peppers, or regional spice blends

- **Cross-Contamination**—A safety hazard involving the transfer of bacteria from one surface to another; common with raw meat

- **Dressing**—Stuffing that cooked outside of a bird and served in a side dish

- **Dutch Oven**—A large, versatile pot with thick walls that is suitable for a variety of cooking methods

- **Extra Virgin Olive Oil**—The highest quality of olive oil

- **Finishing Sauce**—A sauce added to a recipe in the final stage of cooking, or served alongside the meal as a dipping sauce

- **Five Spice Powder**—A spice blend incorporating five different spices, usually (but not always) consisting of cloves, anise, cinnamon, fennel, and cracked black pepper

- **Flavor Injector**—A kitchen gadget similar to a large syringe used to inject various ingredients into meat

- **Flavor Profile**—The combination of tastes and aromas in a particular food

- **Fusion Food**—Food that combines elements from two or more different cuisines